THE GEARS FOR GROOVING ON DRUMSET

MB22184

BY BILL "STUHLLY" BRENNENSTUHL

Visit us on the Web at www.melbay.com or www.billsmusicshelf.com

Contents

Chapter 1   Page

Basic motion: Down/Up — 1
Exercises 1 Down/Up — 1
Exercise 2 Single Hand Roll — 2
Rudiment Study: — 3
Single stroke Roll — 3
Double Stroke Roll — 3
Paradiddle — 4
Flam — 5
Exercise 3 Single Stroke to Flam — 5
Exercise 4 double Stroke to Alternating Flam — 6
Drum set timing and Motion: Down /Up — 7
Basic groove 8ths in HH and BD — 8
Basic Groove: BD Variations — 8
Basic Groove: 8ths in HH 16th variations in BD — 11
Basic Groove: 8ths in HH/ BD 8ths and 16ths variations — 12
Basic Groove: 16th note Lead w/ mixed BD — 15

Chapter 2

Basic Motion: Down/Bounce/Up — 19
Single hand triplet roll — 20
Single Stroke Roll (triplet Feel) — 20
Rudiment Study: — 21
3 Stroke Roll — 21
Flam Tap — 22
Exercise 5: 3stroke roll to Flam Tap — 22
Flam Accent — 23
Basic Groove: The 6/8 Feel — 24
Basic Groove: The Shuffle — 26
Basic Groove: 3 note 16th patterns on the HH/ BD Variations (Down/Bounce/Up/ rest) — 30
Basic Groove Up/REST/Down/Bounce BD Variations — 33
Basic Groove: Ghost notes in the Snare Drum — 37
8th HH/ 16th Ghost/ BD Variations — 37
Basic Groove: 3 note 16ths in HH/ Ghost Notes/ BD Variations — 43
Basic Groove: Shuffle Ghost Notes — 47
Chapter Summary — 48

Rudiment Study   **51**
Flam Paradiddle   **51**
Exercise 6: 4 Stroke Alternating roll into Flam Paradiddle   51
Syncopations and The Art of Building a Fill   **52**
Syncopated Listening   **52**
Exercise 7: The 6 stroke roll   53
The Linear 6 Stroke Roll   55
Exercise 7: The Ruff   56
Adding The Flam to Syncopation   57
The 26 Standard American Rudiments   **58**
#1 The Single Stroke Roll   58
#2 The Double Stroke Roll   58
#3 5 Stroke   59
#4 7 Stroke   59
#5 9 Stroke   60
#6 10 Stroke   60
#7 11 Stroke   61
#8 13 Stroke   61
#9 15 Stroke   61
#10 The Paradiddle   62
#11 The Double Paradiddle   62
#12 The Triple Paradiddle   63
#13 The Flam   63
#14 The Flam Tap   64
#15 The Flam Accent   65
#16 The Flam Paradiddle   65
#17 The Flamacue   65
#18 The Ruff   66
#19 The Drag   67
#20 The Double Drag   67
#21 The Drag Paradiddle   68
#22 The Double Drag Paradiddle   68
#23 The Ratamacue   68
#24 The Double Ratamacue   69
#25 Lesson 25   69
#26 The Triple Ratamacue   70

PREFACE

The though for writing this book is to make a complete guide for a system of drumming comprising body motions and transferring them to the drum set. Through my many years of playing I've realized that the natural motion of my body gave me feel on the drums. The Down/Up motion of my arms and wrists and feet translated directly to my timing, feel and power on the drums. By letting these motions flow uninhibited I gained a solid understanding of feel, groove and speed/fluidity around the set. The motions are found in various different well-known techniques and I'm not claiming to originate them, but through the study of these concepts and thoughts you can see the direct link between the down/up motions and timing w/ the metronome, which is a problem spot for most drummers. No more will you chase the click but rather feel it through the motions presented in this system.
The student will learn the way to internalize the metronome, leading to internal feel. This is why it's called grooving because the internal rhythms just flow out of the body without thought. It becomes more instinctual than mental and timing becomes second nature.

Chapter I

Basic Motion: DOWN/UP

The key to grooving and timing is in the lead hand. The lead hand is the hand you play on the HH or Ride cymbal and needs to have a solid flow. This first section will deal with the basic 2 note or Eighth note pattern using a Down/Up motion. First practice the motions on the practice pad as an exercise, then to the drum set as music.

EXERCISE 1: The Down/UpStroke

DOWN STROKE
As you can see in the photo the arm goes down, the stick hits the drum, let the stick rebound up setting the stick up for the return (up) stroke

UP STROKE
The Up Stroke is when the stick moves down to hit the drum as the arm moves UP. The secret to the sequence is allowing the stick to move freely within the hand.

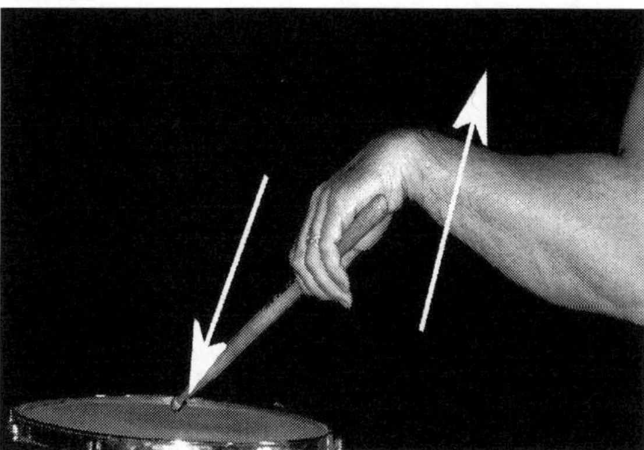

EXERCISE 2: SINGLE HAND ROLL

This exercise will give you the technique needed to accomplish the Single Hand
Roll. Here's how to do it: First let the stick flow freely in your hand you're looking
for a solid even flow. Adjust the fulcrum (the point where your thumb and
forefinger hold the stick) to attain more speed. The loose fulcrum is good for slow
tempo, the faster you go the smaller the fulcrum point gets. But never clinch the
stick tight always have loose hands. The faster you go the more it feels like
dribbling a basketball.
Start with your lead hand then work on your snare hand:

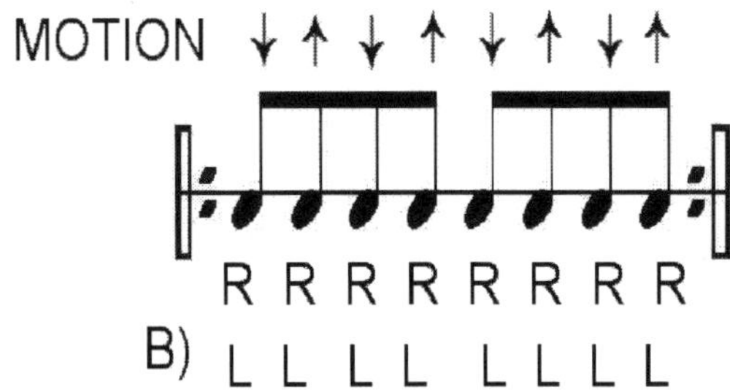

Here' the symbols that'll be used for the Arm/Wrist Motion throughout the book:

ARM/WRIST MOTION:

DOWN ↓   UP ↑ BOUNCE ● FULL ↕ ACCENTED DOWN ↓

Rudiment Study:

The first 4 rudiments you'll study employ the Down/Up strokes in different combinations. Mastering these will give you a great foundation to build upon.

#1 The Single Stroke Roll

The one, the only Single Stroke Roll. The single stroke is used to sync up the down/up strokes in each hand. You're going to start with 2 down Strokes then 2 Up Strokes then repeat. Start with your lead hand first then stop and do the opposite hand lead.

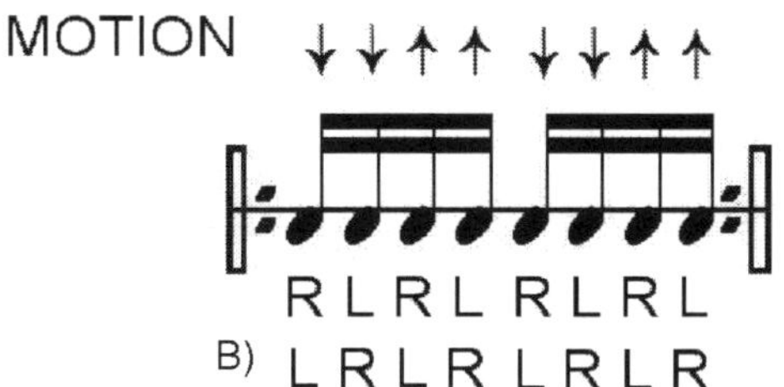

#2 The Double Stroke Roll

The second most commonly used rudiment. Playing it open you'll have the fulcrum loose. The faster you go the more the fulcrum tightens. To create the Buzz Roll just tighten the fulcrum on the Down stroke then release for the Up.

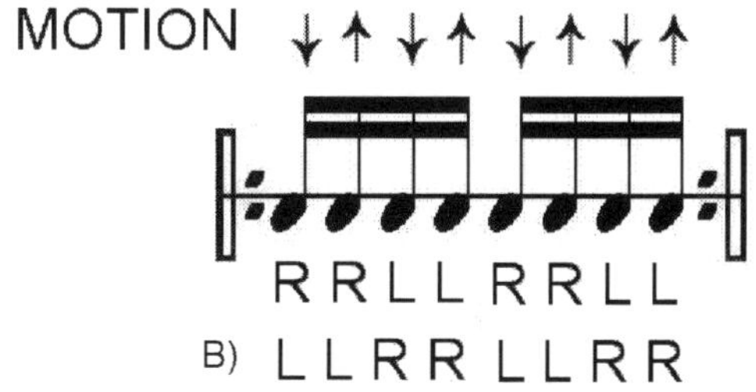

Fulcrum Exercise:

The secret to a great double stroke roll is being able to bounce the strokes. With this exercise you'll play a down/up then rest and repeat. To go faster squeeze the fulcrum on the down stroke then release. DO NOT tighten the hand/arm/wrist always remain loose.

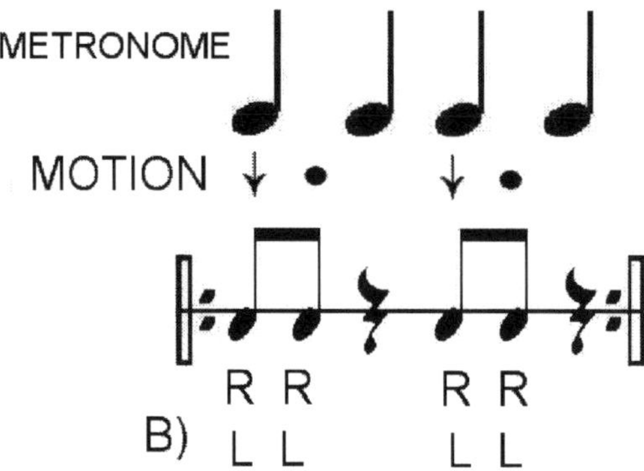

#3 The Paradiddle

Another commonly known rudiment it combines the single stroke and double stroke motions. Start with a DOWN stroke ACCENT in the R.H letting it rebound up making it a FULL stroke, then an UP stroke in the L.H. and finally a double using Down and a BOUNCE stroke, which is letting the rebound hit without returning the motion UP . Then reverse the sequence starting with the LH.

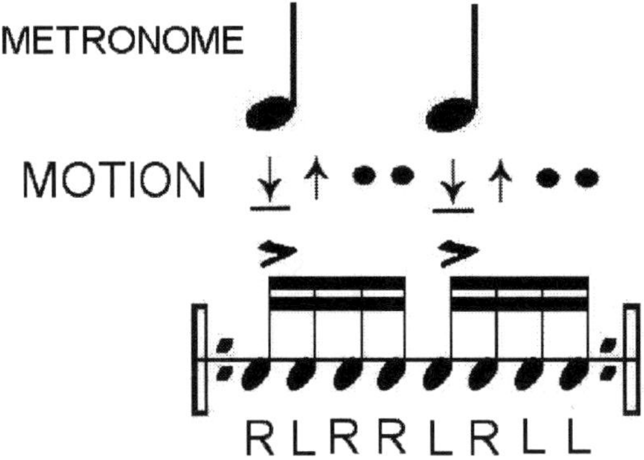

#4 The Flam

The best way to explain The Flam is this way: It's the exact same motion as the single stroke roll but rhythmically uneven. The first note is an accendental, meaning it has no rhythmical value. The height of the first note is closer to the drumhead. The second note is the rhythm, for this example it'll be a quarter note.

Non- Alternating: as you can see the motion is exactly the same just the RH plays a fraction before the LH which is on the beat.

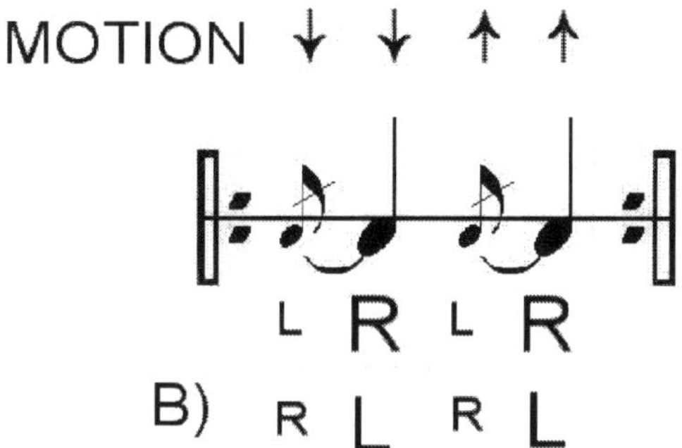

EXERCISE 3: SINGLE STROKE TO FLAM

This exercise or Hybrid rudiment will help you learn the Flam and tighten your single stroke Roll

Alternating

Start with an UP stroke and a DOWN stroke staggered. The smaller note rebounds up to set you up for the next note. When you pick up speed it feels exactly like a Double Stroke Roll Flamming.

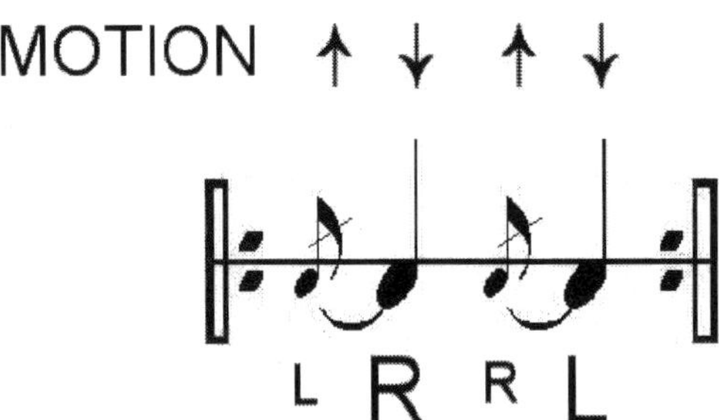

Here's an exercise to help with the execution of the Alternating Flam:

EXERCISE 4: DOUBLE STROKE ROLL TO ALTERNATING FLAM

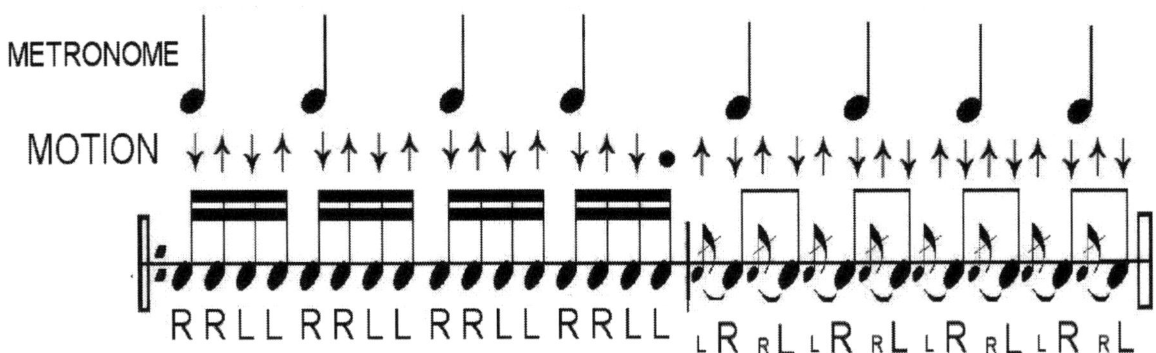

Drum set Timing and Motion

Drumming is dancing! That basic thought process will allow you to free up the thought of timing and get down to the basics of what make a great drummer! In this section you'll explore the basic motions that will allow you to play better time today.

The key to this exercise is to lock in the DOWN strokes on the HH/Ride with the metronome. The Lead Hand (HH) moves Down and Up. The snare drum (SN) hits together with the HH Down w/ a full stroke.
Here's how this motion will look as music.

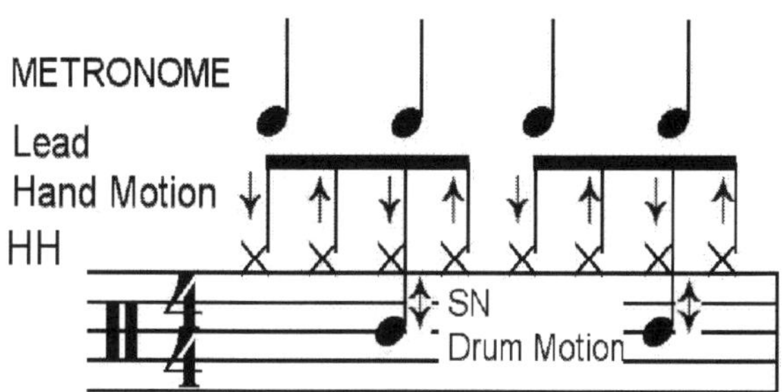

Play this exercise starting @ 60 BPM and repeat until locking into the metronome. Now that the hand movements are addressed, we add the BD.

Basic groove: 8ths in HH and BD

The key to perfect timing is playing a ton and varying the movements using exercises. Here' we'll move the BD around to create different grooves. Remember to lock into the metronome, relax and let the notes flow out.

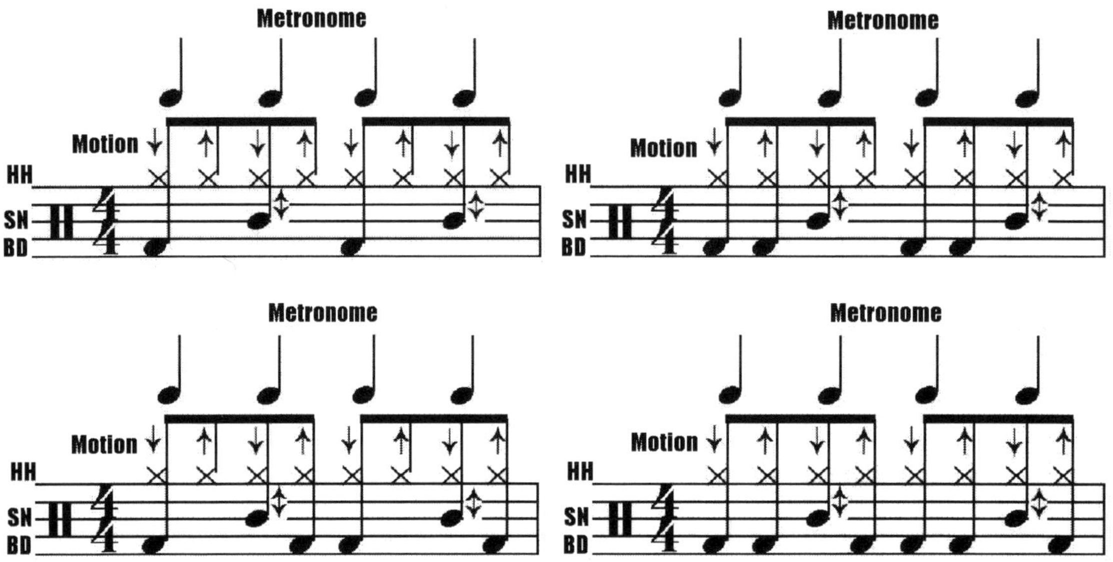

Basic Groove: BD Variations

These 4 grooves are the basics that we'll now expand on. REMEMBER: Practice with the metronome and lock in the lead hand.

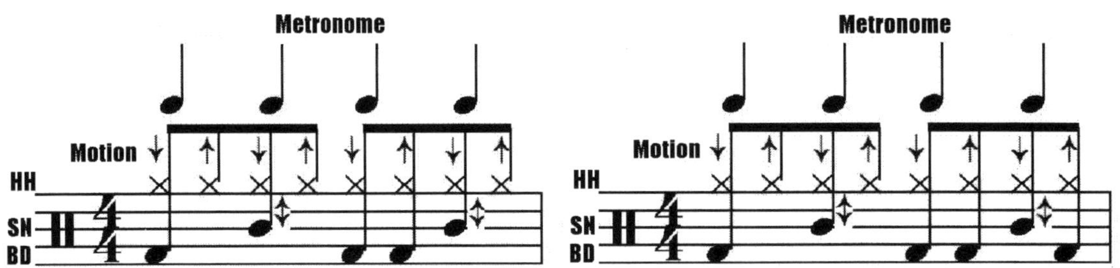

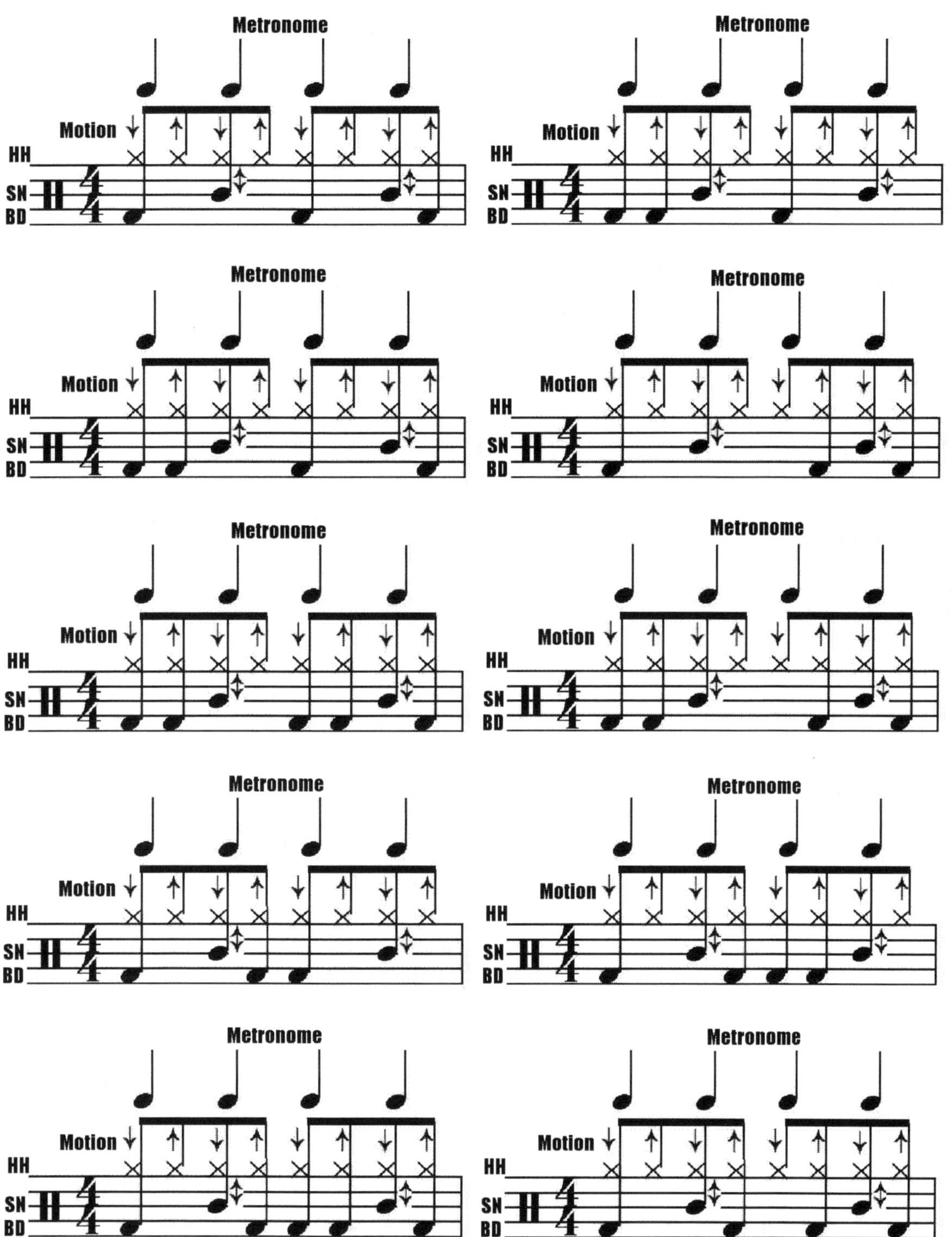

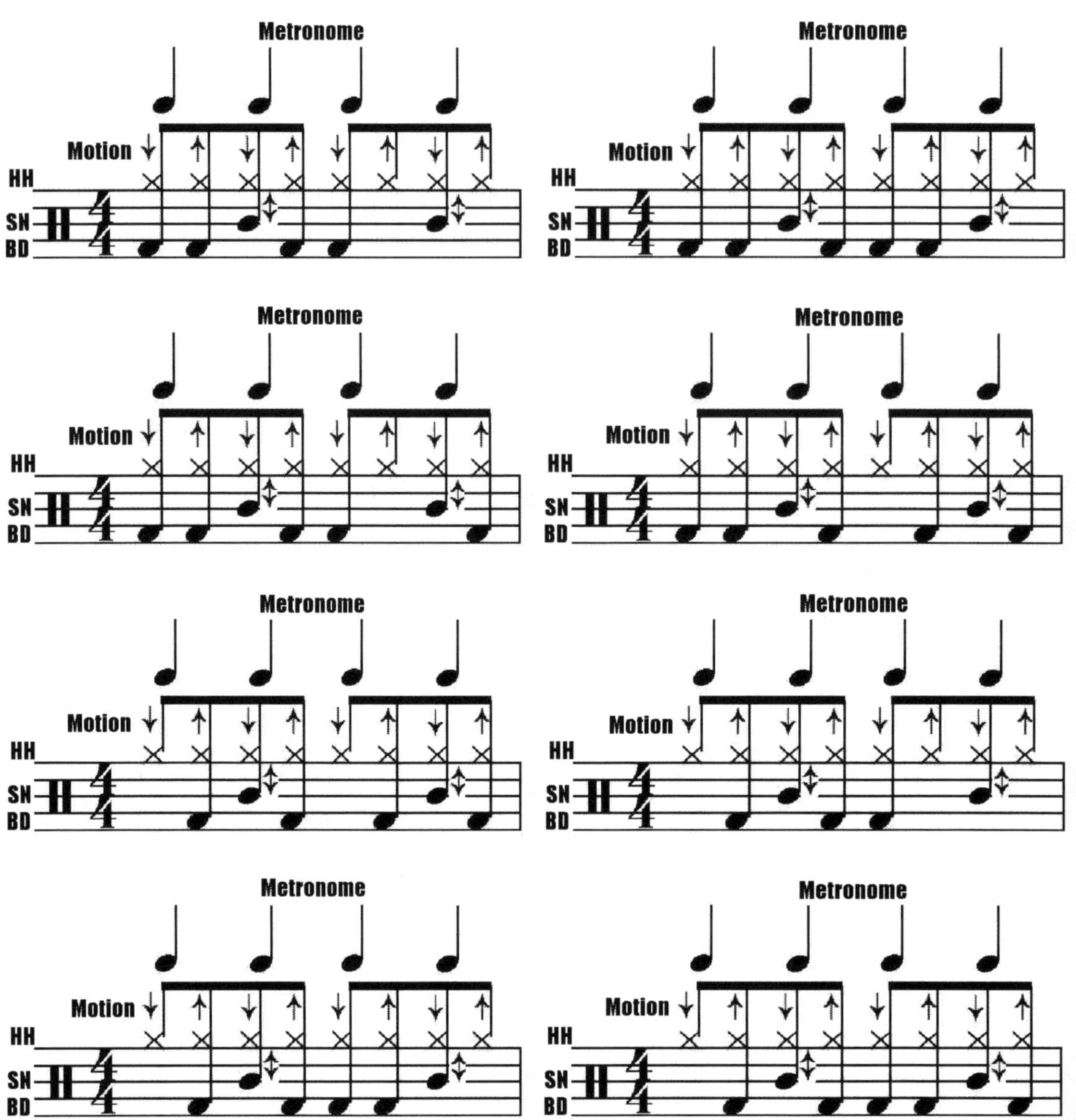

Basic groove: 8th notes in the H.H./ 16th note BD variations

Now we'll add 16th in the BD with the Down/Up 8th note HH. The 16th note drops in between the 8ths giving it a galloping feel. I'll write the metronome and the 16th note rhythm so you can line the beats up properly

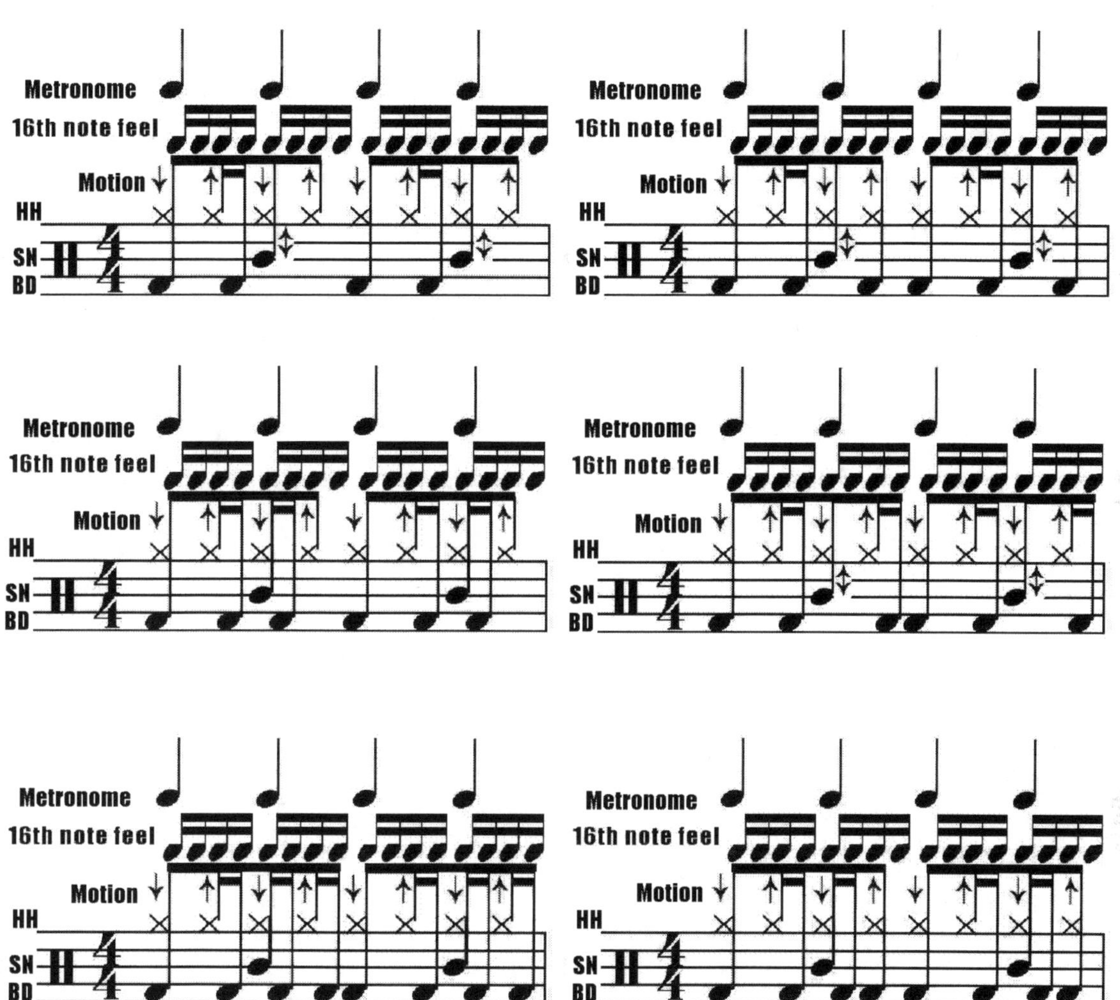

Basic Groove: 8ths in HH/ BD 8ths and 16ths variations

In these next grooves you'll be switching from 8th note feel to 16th feel in the same measure. to accomplish this correctly sing the metronome as 2 Quarter notes then as the 16th note grouping.

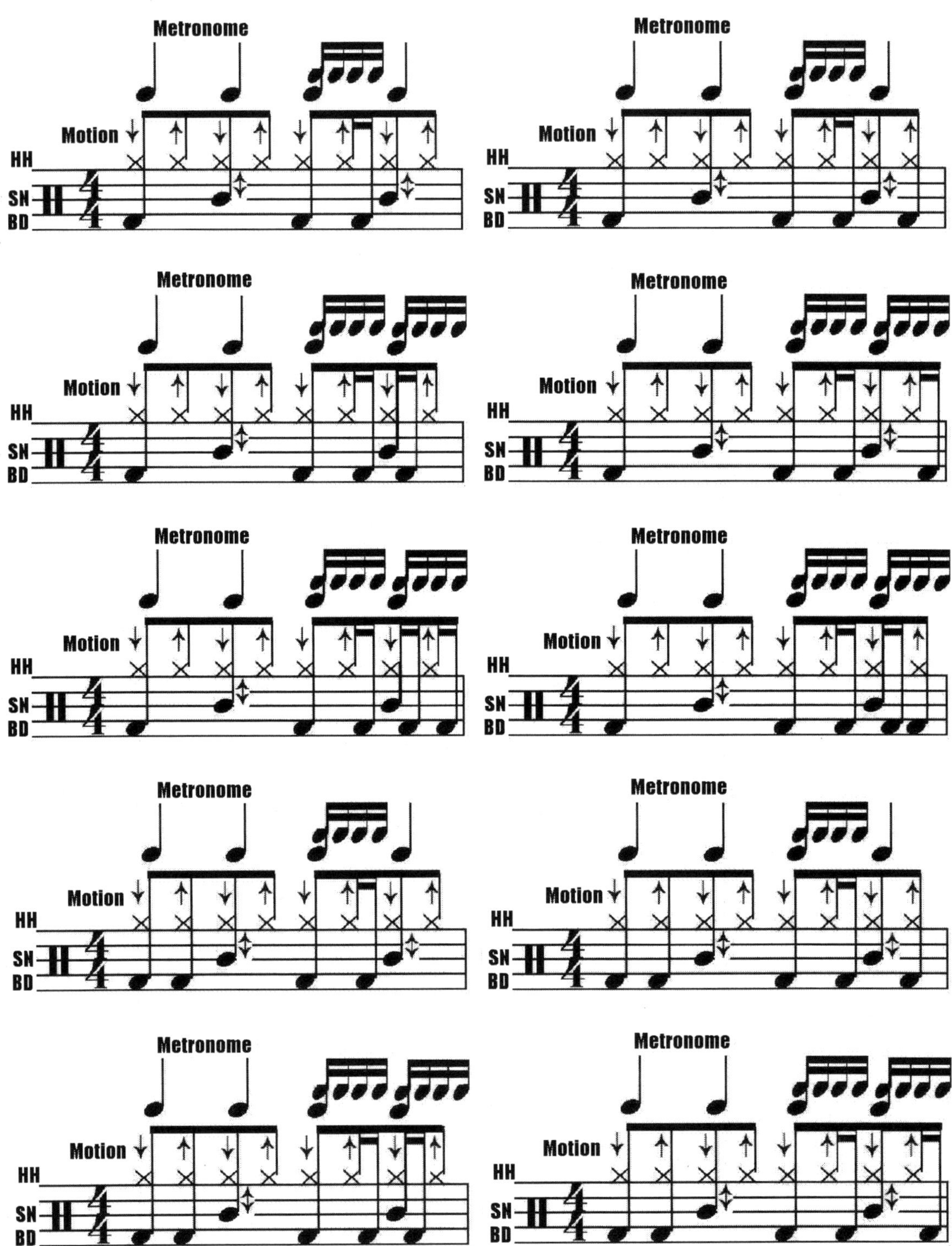

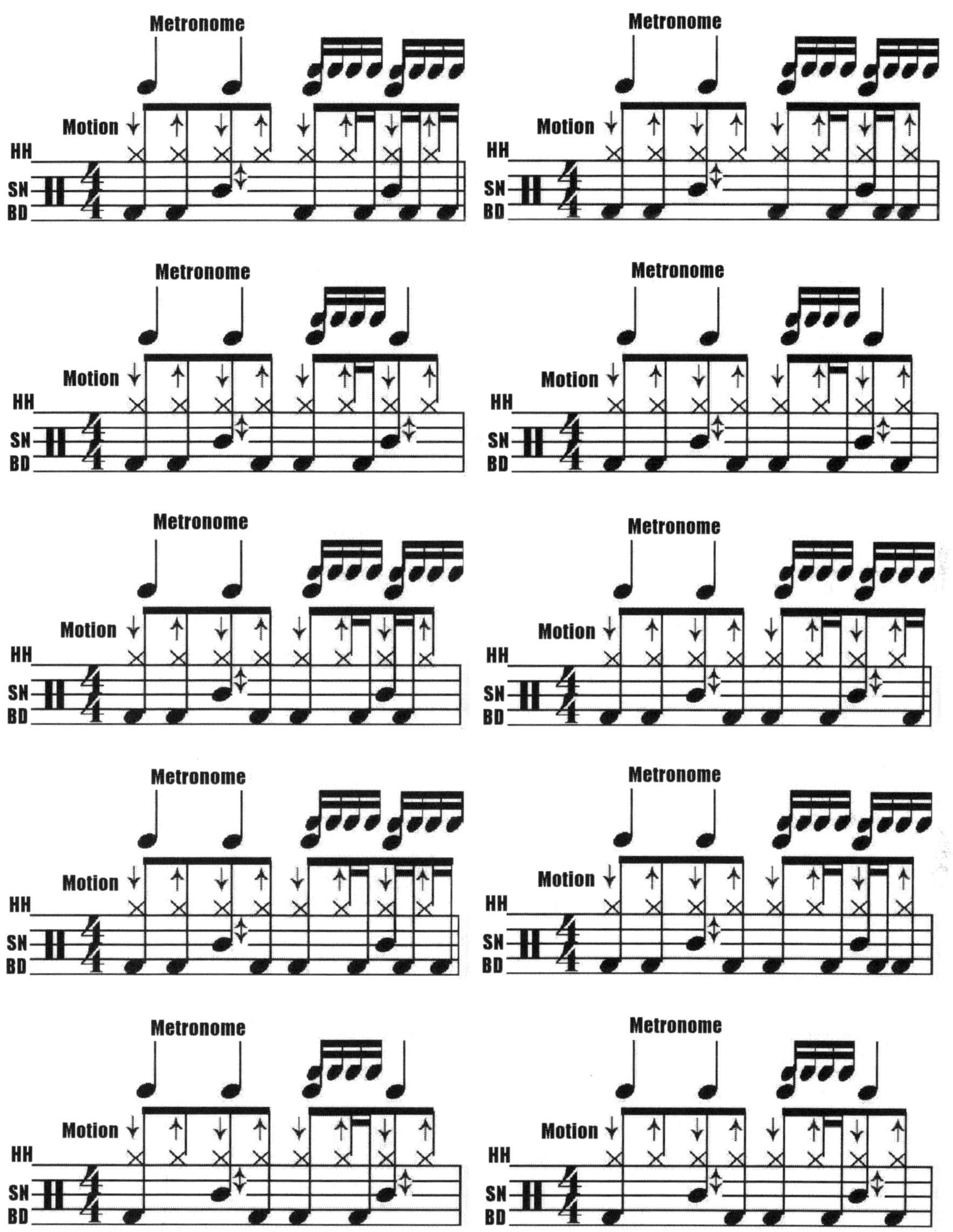

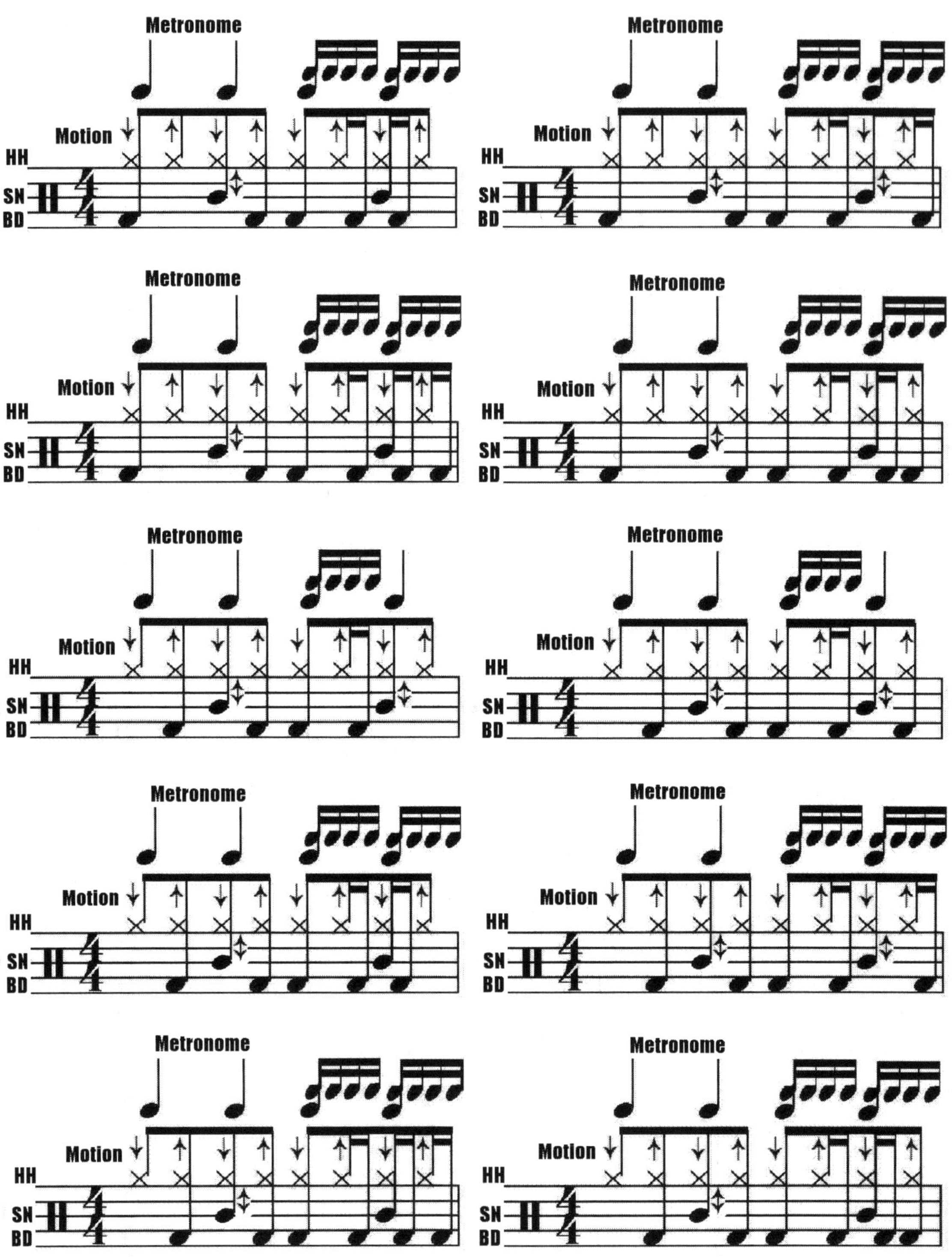

Basic Groove: 16th Note lead w/mixed BD

By now the Down/Up stroke groove should be feeling like a natural movement. Now we'll use the same Down/Up to play double time in the HH with the lead hand or as their commonly known as 16th notes. Follow the motions and lock into the metronome:

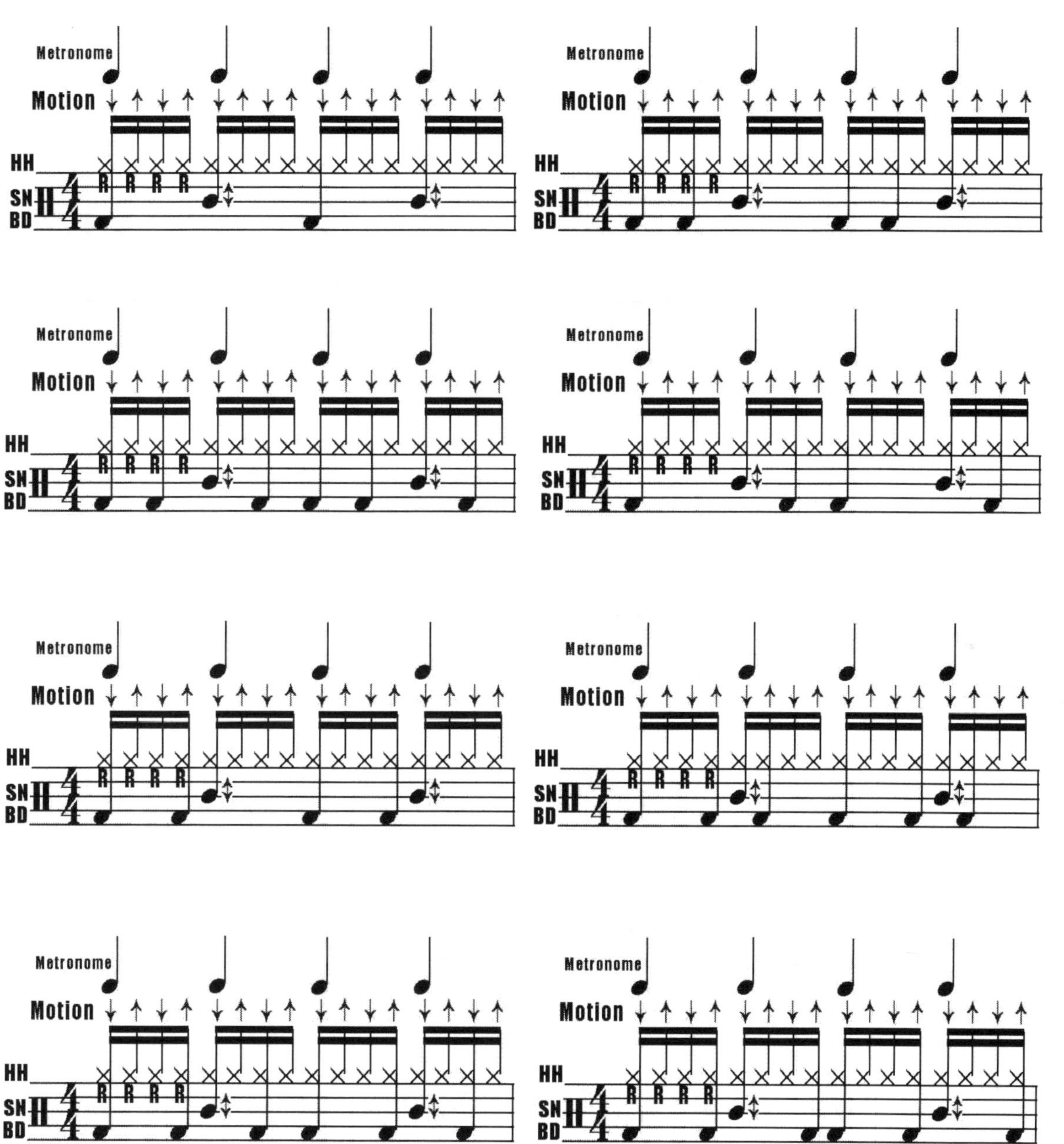

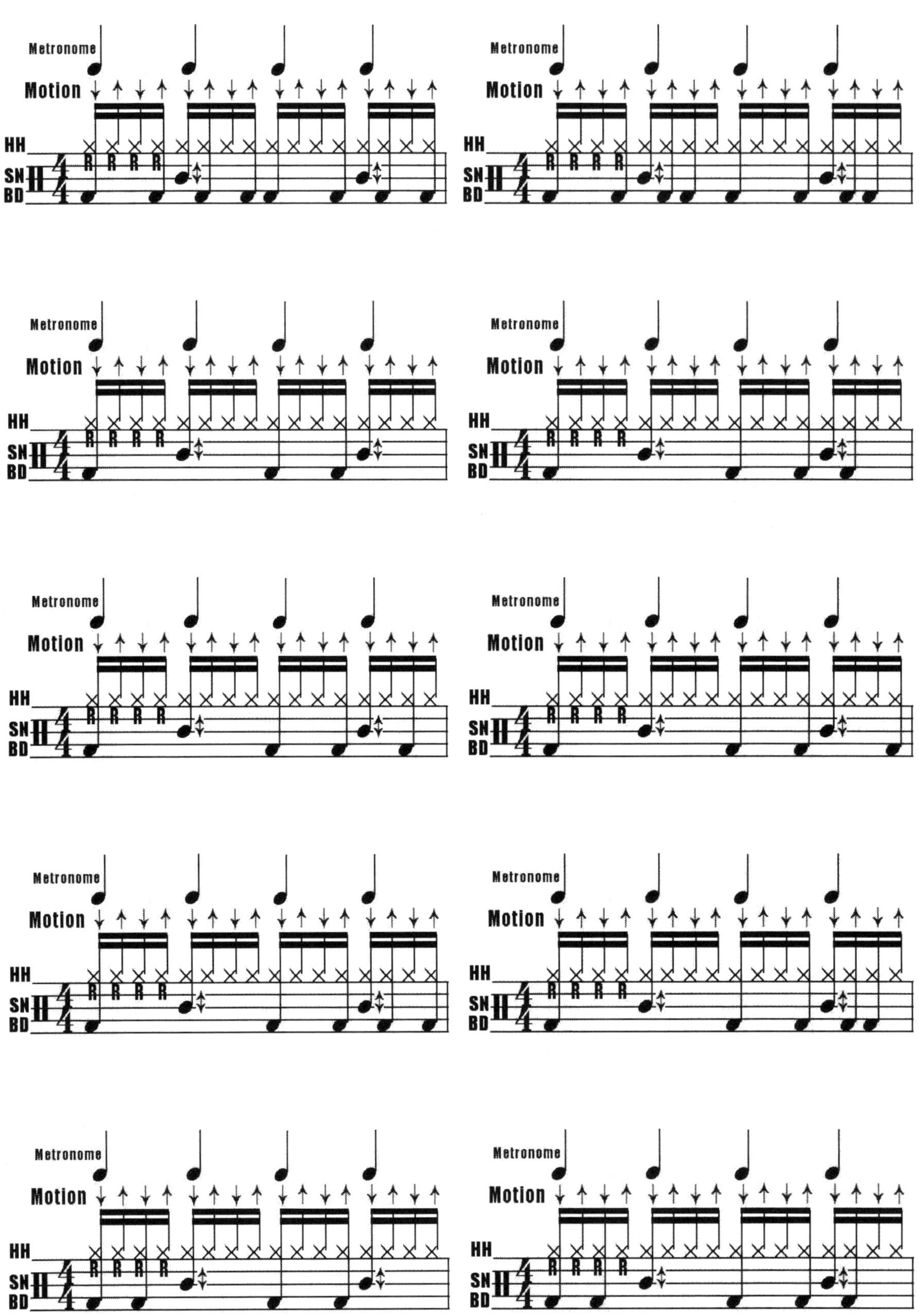

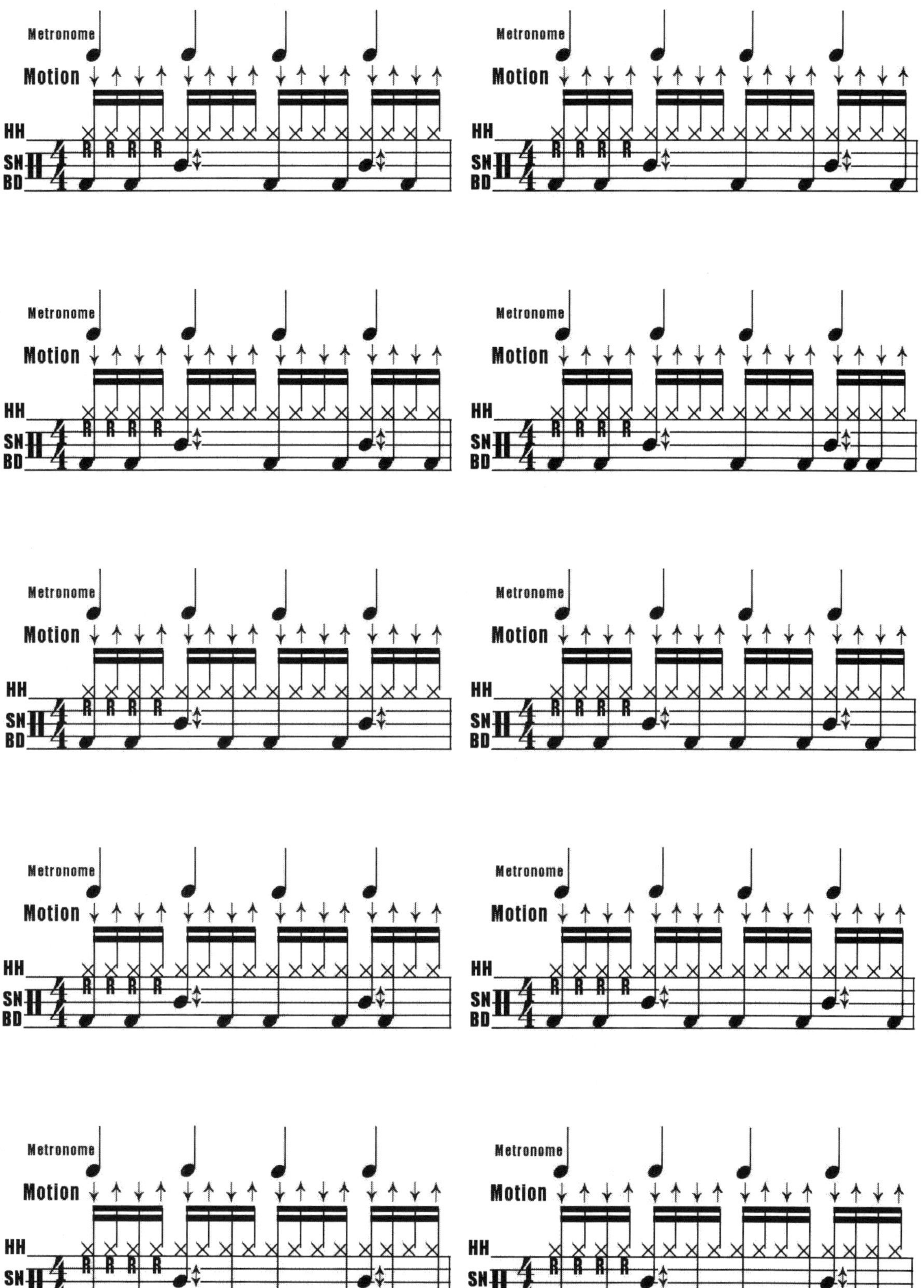

Play the above exercises with this pattern as well:

Chapter 2

Basic Motion: Down/Bounce/Up

In this next group of exercises we're going to use the bounce stroke. To achieve the **BOUNCE** stroke you'll freeze you hand in position and let the rebound drop to simply let the stick bounce. The **BOUNCE** uses the rebound but you're not resetting it with an **UP** arm motion
To play a 3 note group you'll start with **1. Down Stroke**. Keeping you hand still let the stick **2. BOUNCE** for the second stroke.

Hit the drum let the stick rebound

Next let it bounce while the hand stays stationary

last stroke(up)when the arm/wrist is resetting

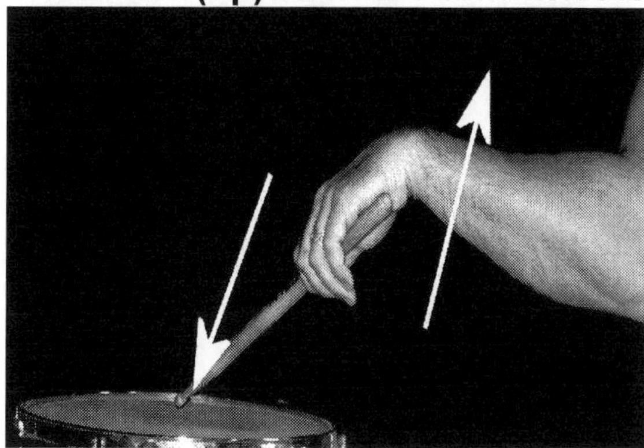

Below is the motions in the diagrams written into music:

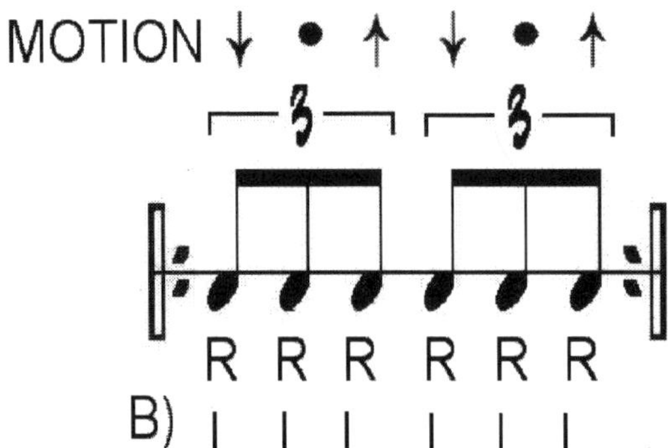

Striving for a fluid steady sound, the faster you go the more the fulcrum tightens to limit the bounce height. Practice this rhythm many times first with the RH then with the LH.

Single Stroke Roll Triplet Base:

The motion in the hands is the same as the single hand exercise. The motion should feel like dribbling a basketball.

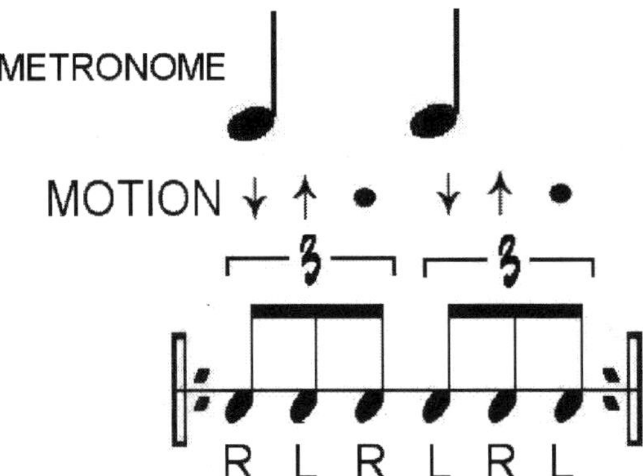

Rudiment Study:

3 Stroke Roll Alternating Hands:

This exercise is similar to the 2 stroke bouncing exercise you did to help with the Double Stroke Roll. REMEMBER don't clinch the stick just squeeze on the fulcrum then release. Always have loose hands:

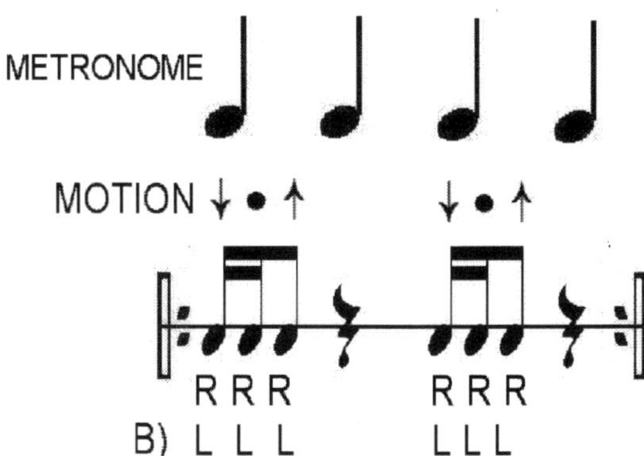

Now incorporate these exercises into the 3 stroke Alternating Roll. The notes should be fluid and even. And as always loose hands:

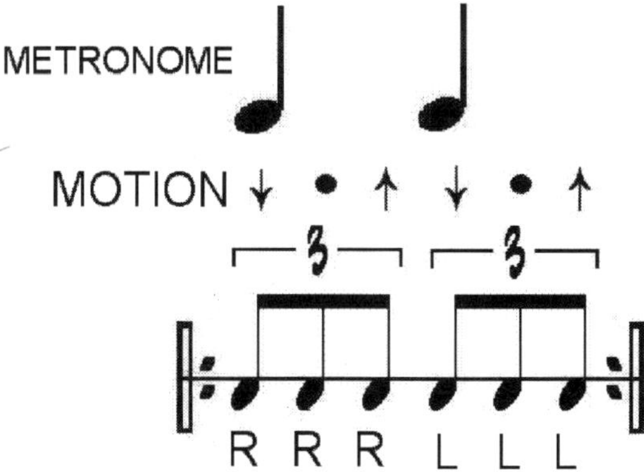

#14 The Flam Tap

The Alternating version is a 3 Stroke Roll staggered into itself.

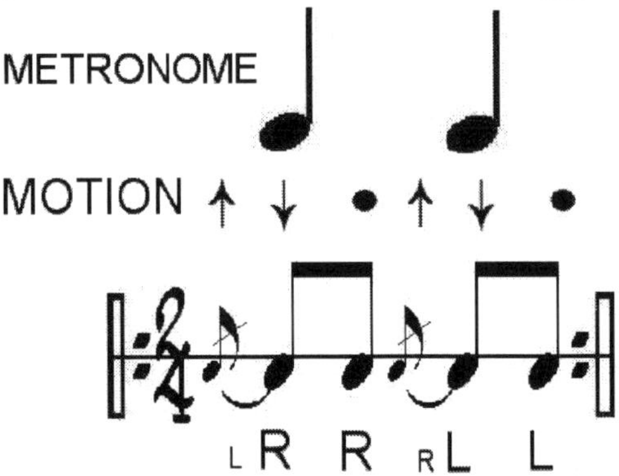

Exercise 5: 3 Stroke Roll to Flam Tap

In this hybrid rudiment the 3 Stroke Roll is use to make to separate rhythmical feels. The rhythm should flow without interruption, but the feel will change.

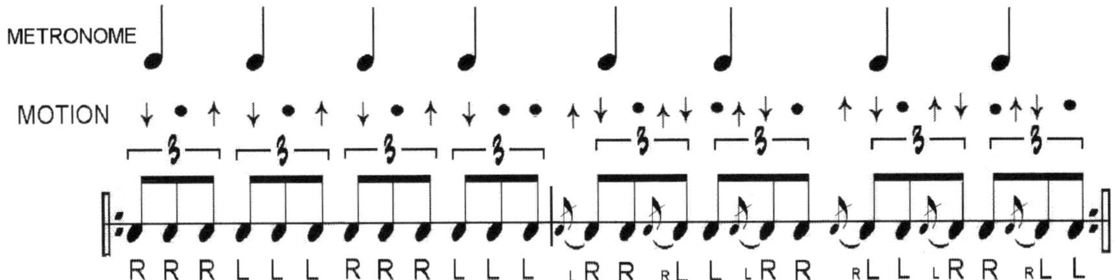

Non-Alternating

This has two DOWN/UP motions going on at the same time. The Flam grace note has the same motion as the main note, but the rhythm of it is a half.

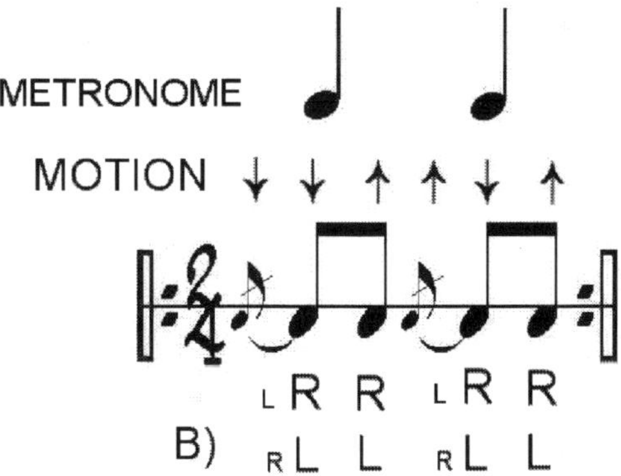

#15 The Flam Accent

This rudiment is an alternating Triplet rhythm with a Flam in the beginning. The 3 note roll is masked by The Flam but studying the 3 note will help with this rudiment.

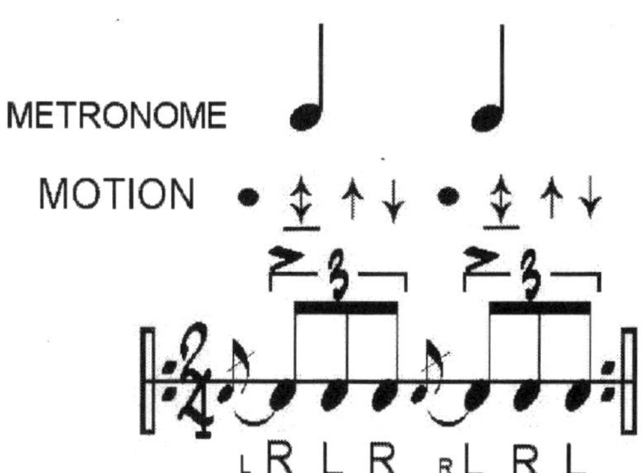

Basic Groove: The 6/8 feel

In this section you'll use the 3 stroke techniques to play grooves in 6/8. You can think of 6/8 as 2 sets of triplets in 2/4. The metronome marking is on the dotted Quarter Note.

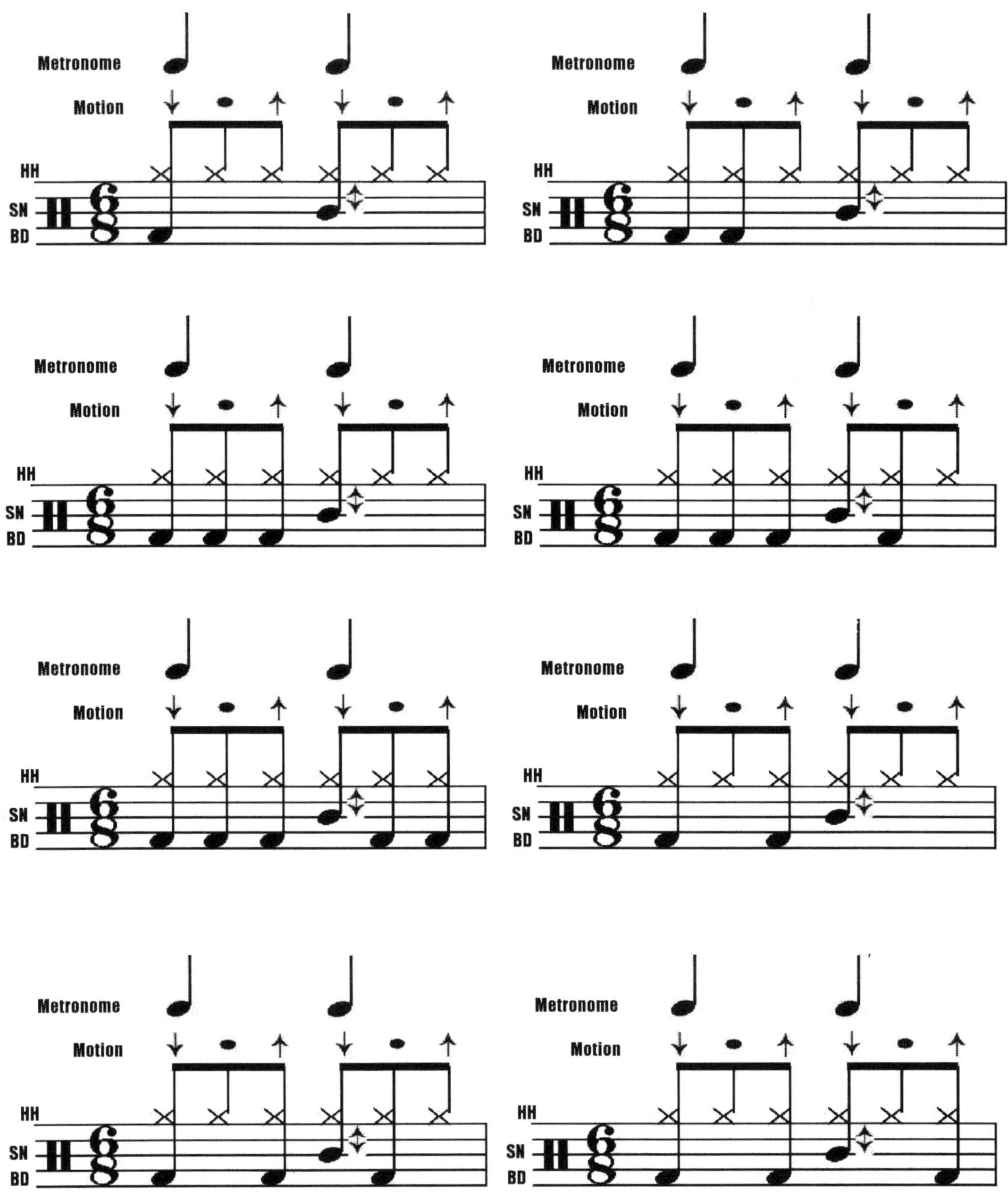

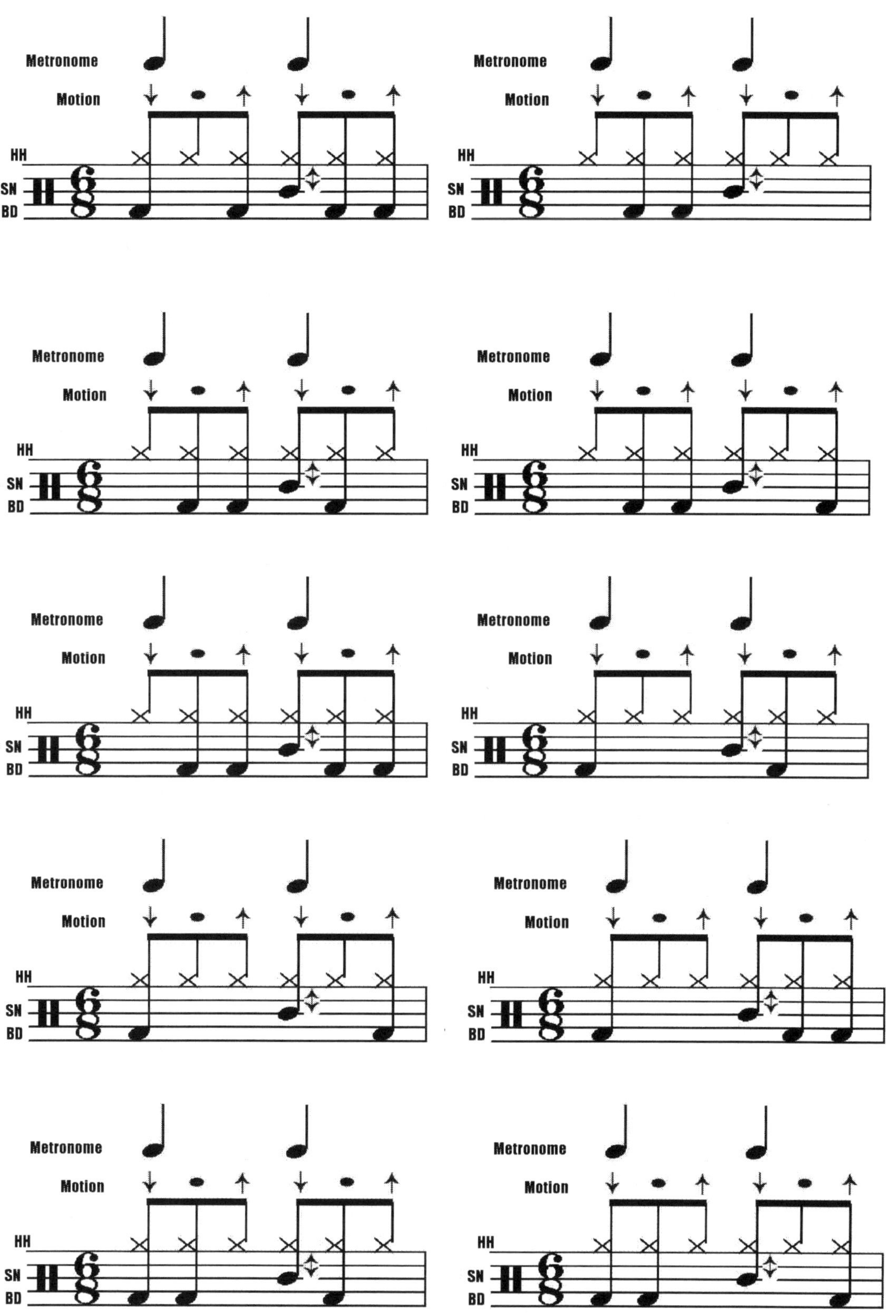

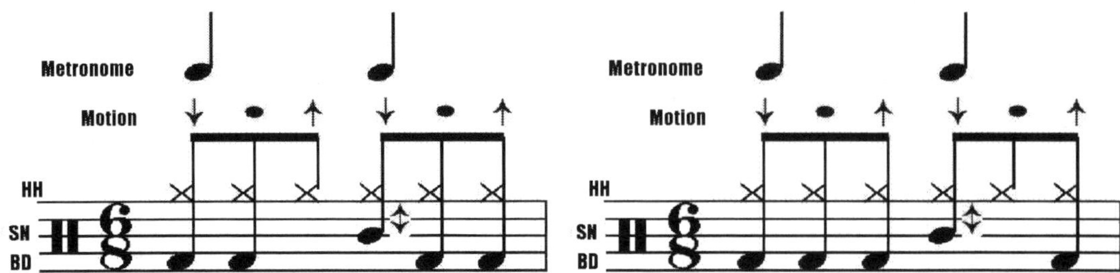

Basic Groove: The Shuffle

The shuffle is based on a triplet feel. The Triplet is superimposed into 2/4 from 6/8 and has a rest on the second beat. Sounds confusing? We'll when you play see it it'll make complete sense. The lead hand will be using the Down/Rest/Up stroke to create the shuffle rhythm.

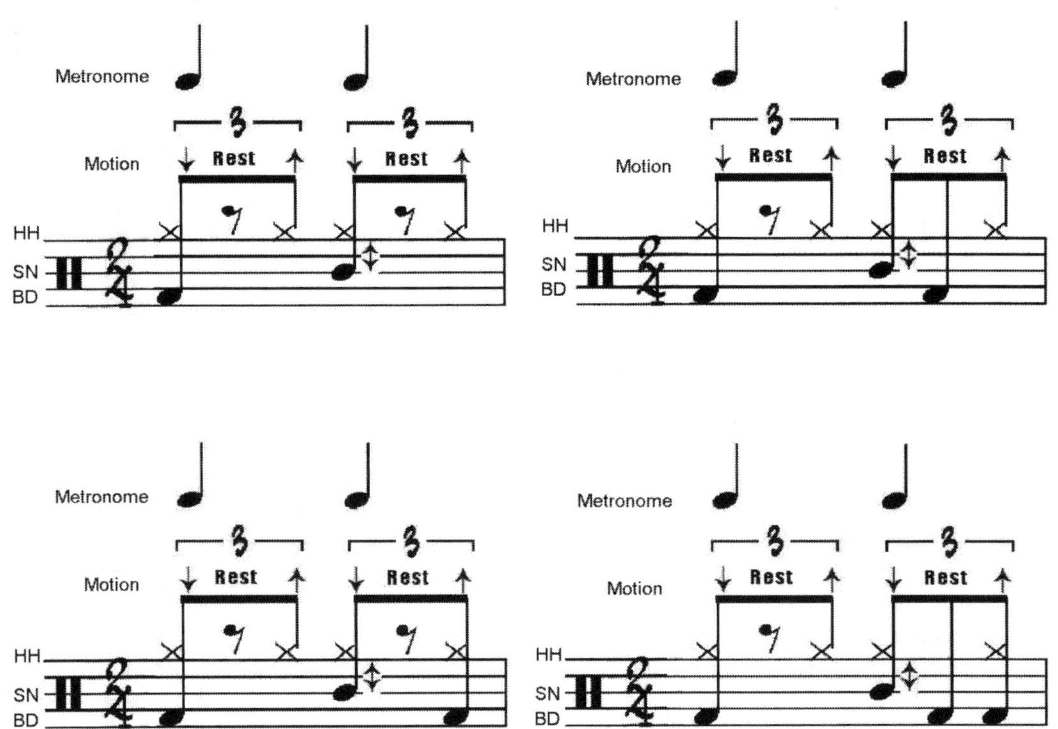

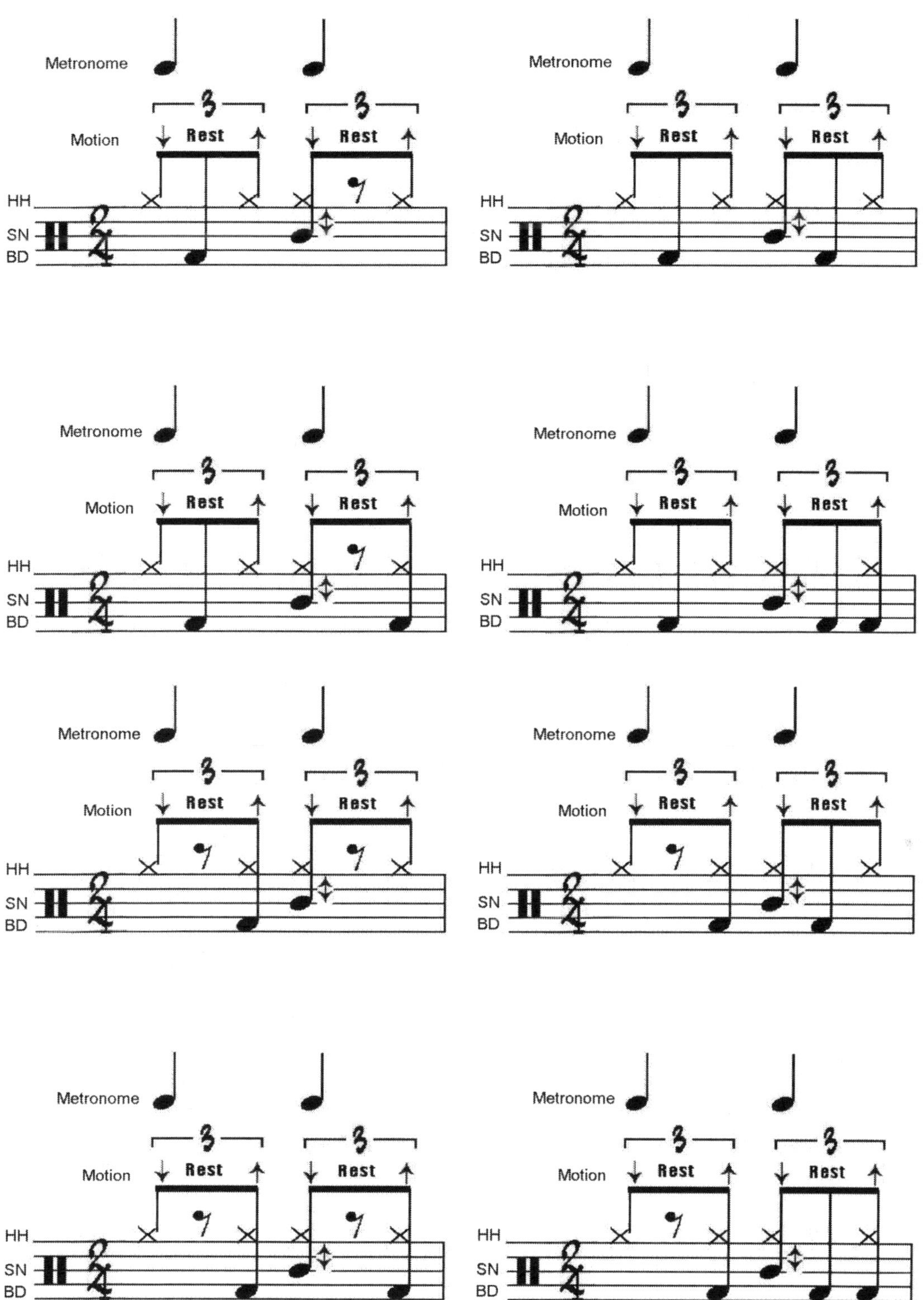

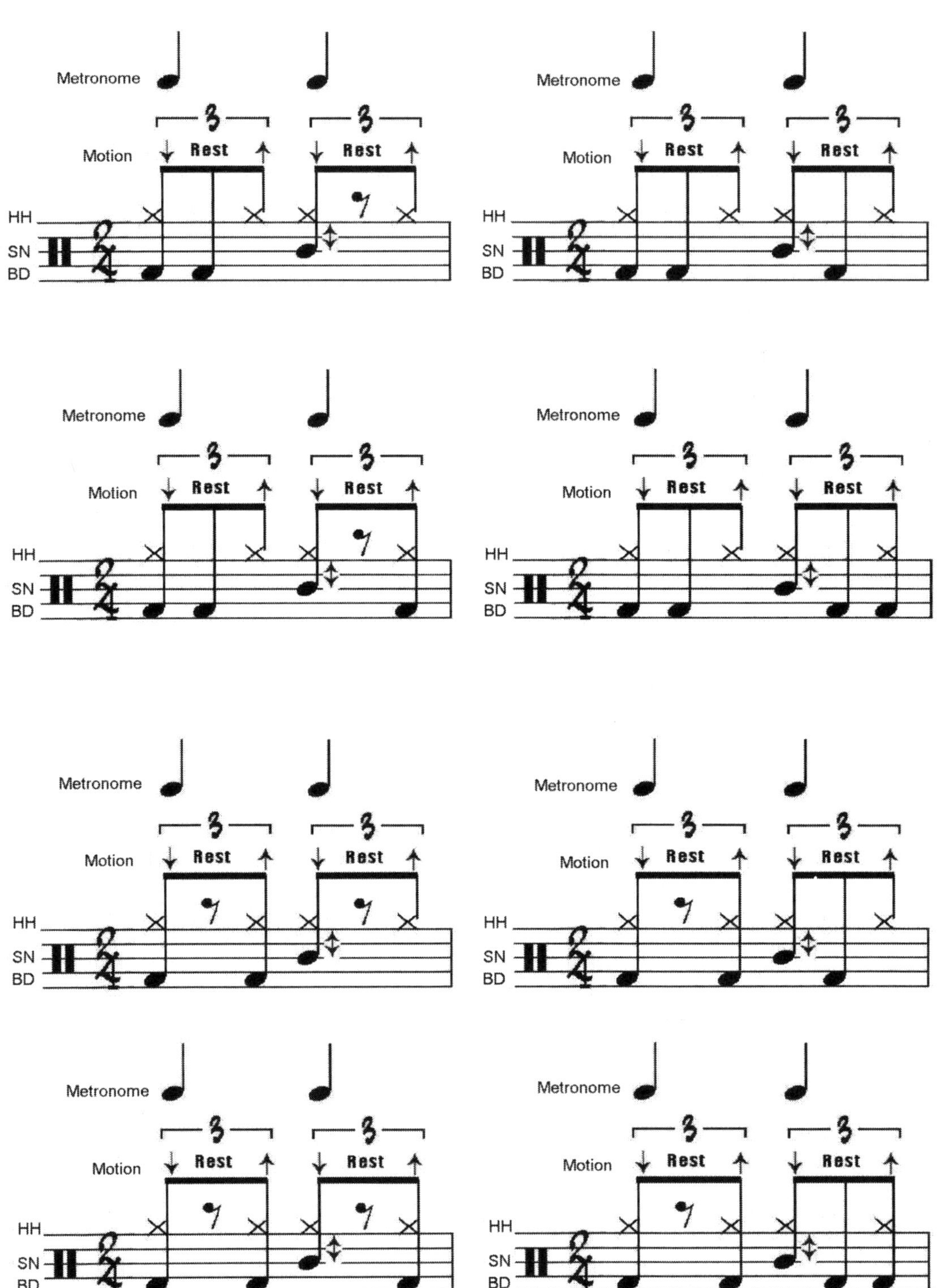

Metronome
Motion
Rest
Rest
HH
SN
BD

Metronome
Motion
Rest
Rest
HH
SN
BD
Metronome
Motion
Rest
Rest
HH
SN
BD
Metronome
Motion
Rest
Rest
HH
SN
BD
Metronome
Motion
Rest
Rest
HH
SN
BD
Metronome
Motion
Rest
Rest
HH
SN
BD
Metronome
Motion
Rest
Rest
HH
SN
BD
Metronome
Motion
Rest
Rest
HH
SN
BD
Metronome
Motion
Rest
Rest
HH
SN
BD

Basic Groove: 3 note 16th Patterns on the HH/ BD Variations

Use the Down/Bounce/Up/Rest strokes in these 16th note broken patterns. You'll have the metronome marking and the 16th breakdown above the grooves to lock in the feel.

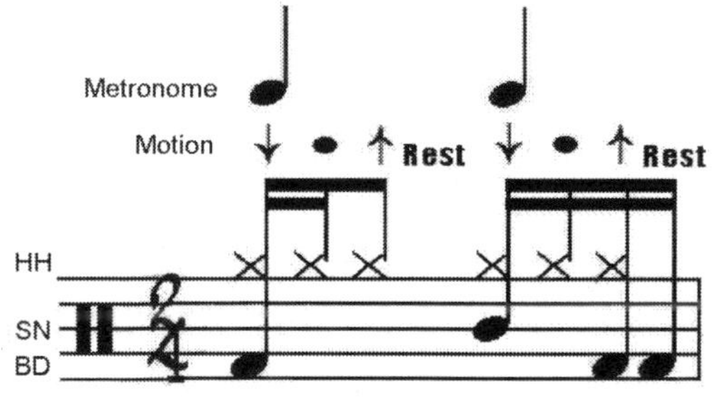
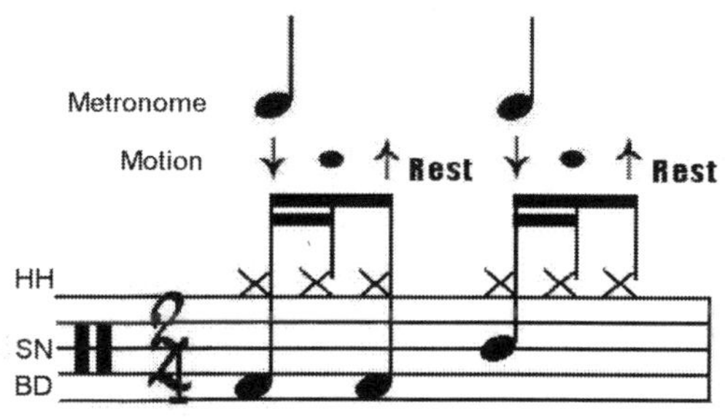

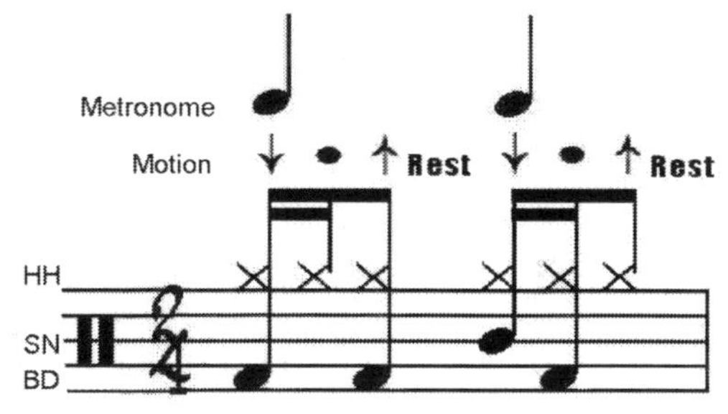
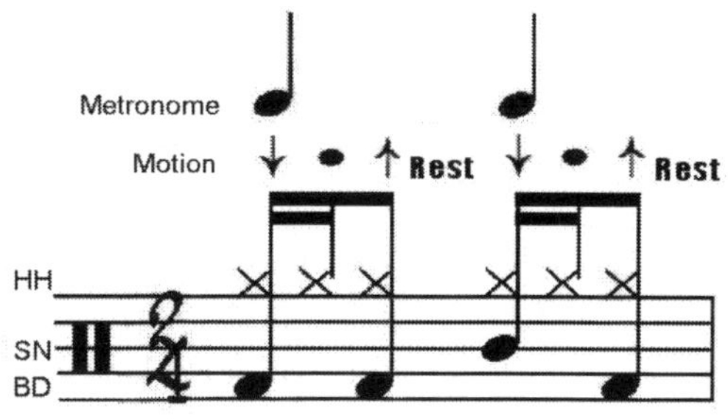

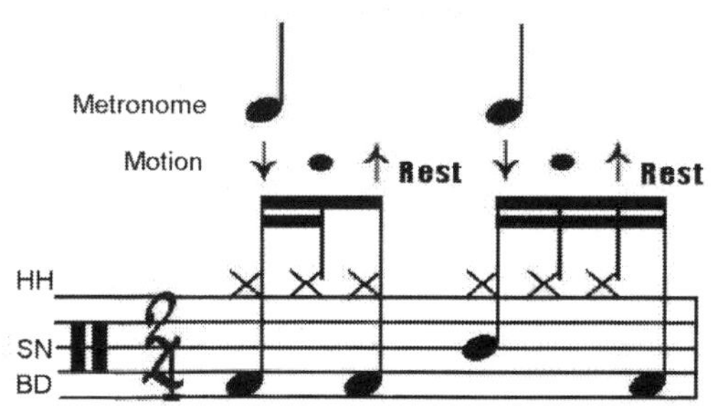
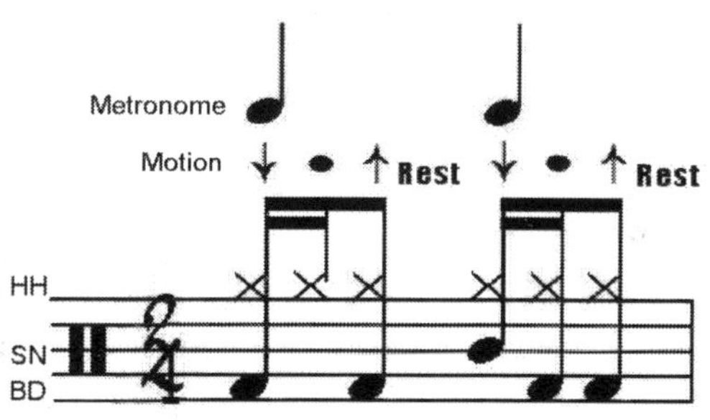

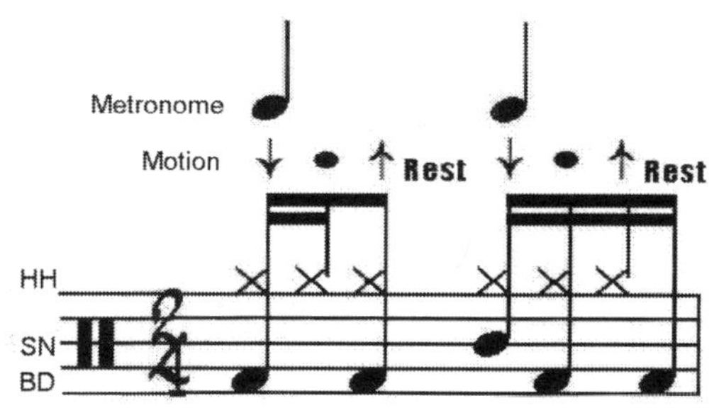
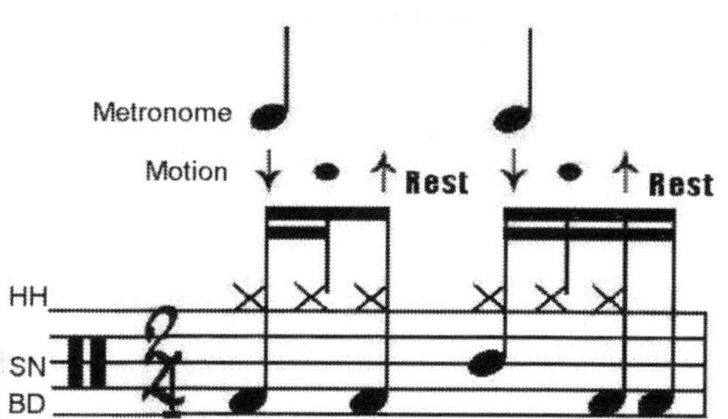

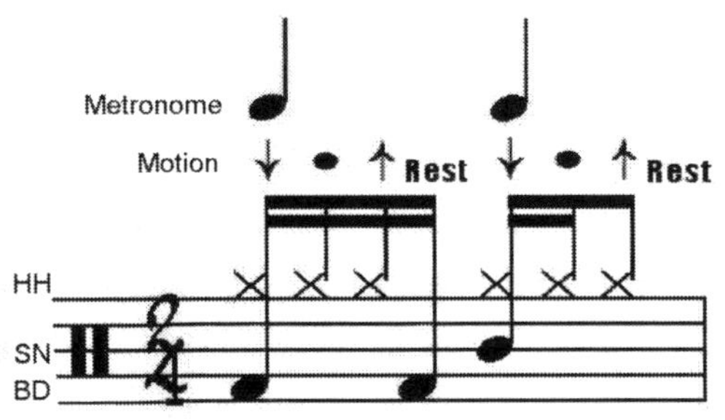

Metronome
Motion
Rest
Rest
HH
SN
BD

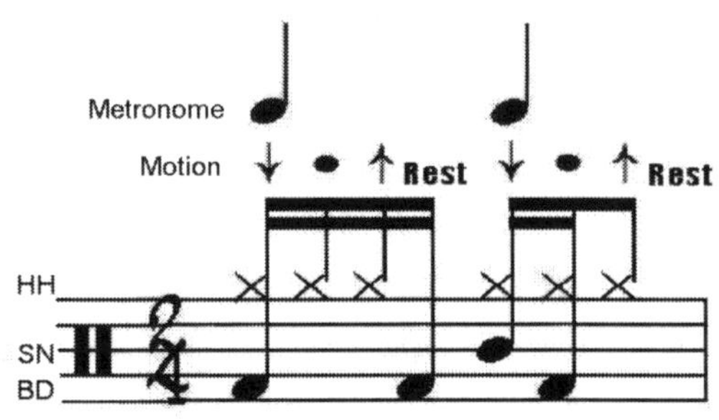

Metronome
Motion
Rest
Rest
HH
SN
BD

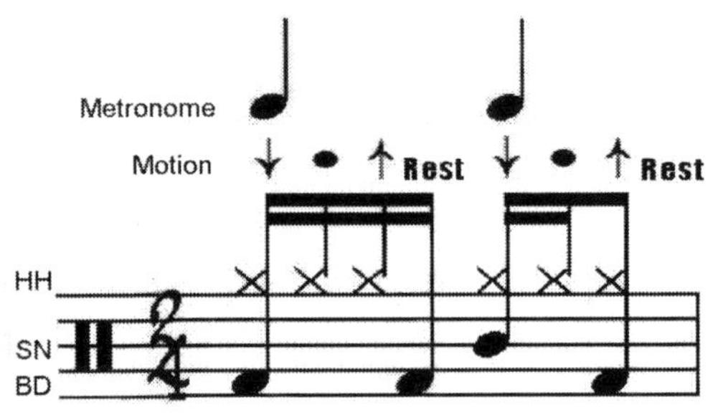

Metronome
Motion
Rest
Rest
HH
SN
BD

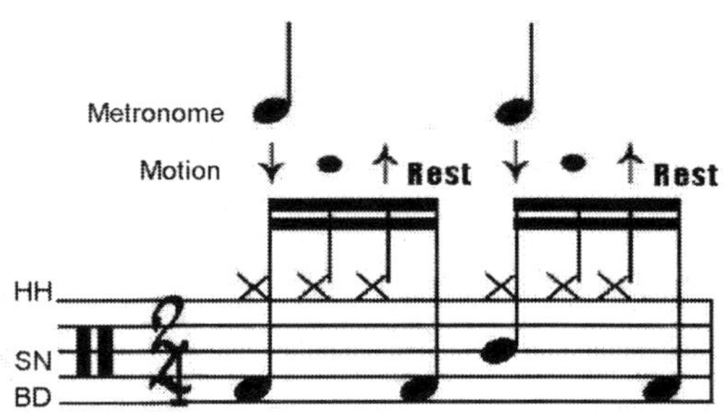

Metronome
Motion
Rest
Rest
HH
SN
BD

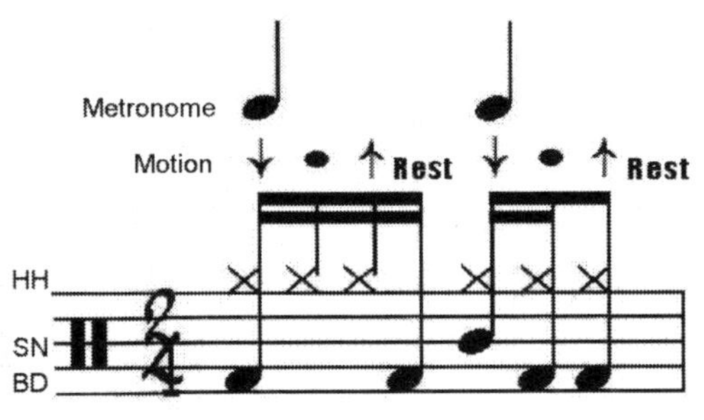

Metronome
Motion
Rest
Rest
HH
SN
BD

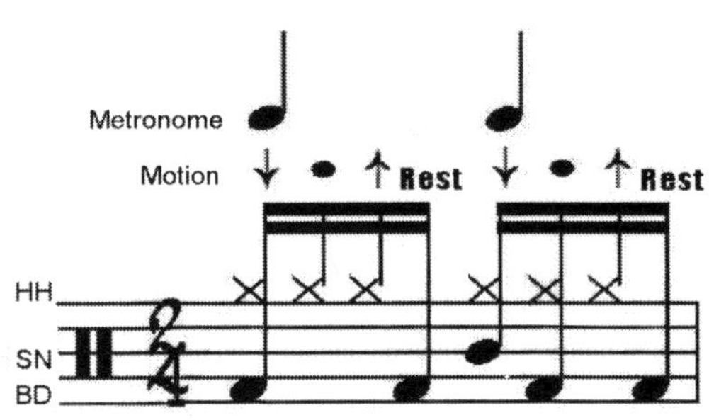

Metronome
Motion
Rest
Rest
HH
SN
BD

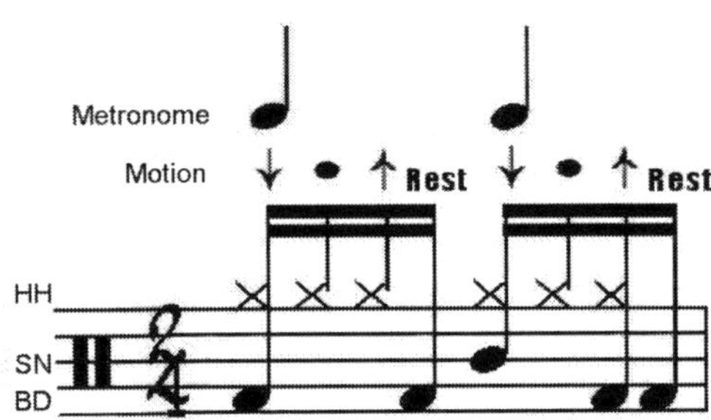

Metronome
Motion
Rest
Rest
HH
SN
BD

Basic Groove: (Up/Rest/Down/Bounce) BD Variations

The same motion is just moved down the line to give an upbeat feel. The rhythmical focus is on the upbeat of the groove.

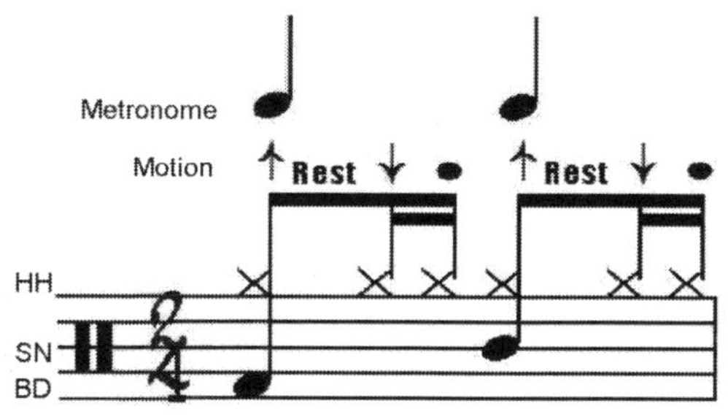

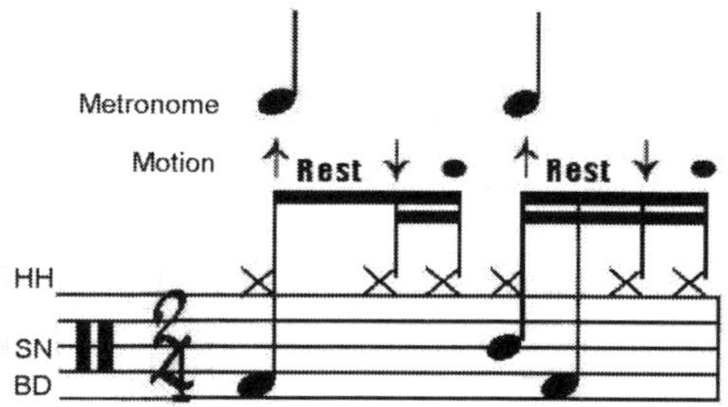

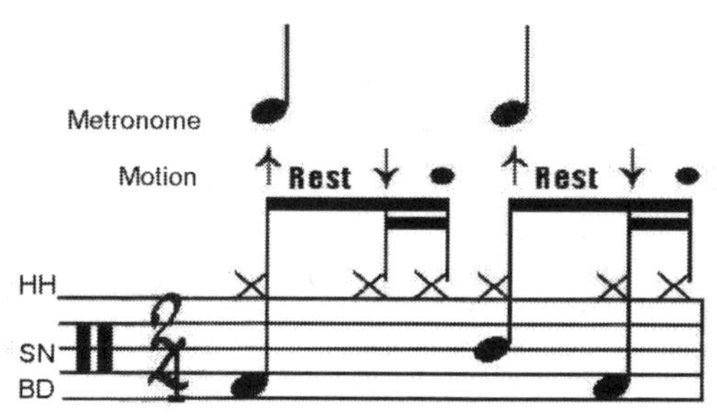

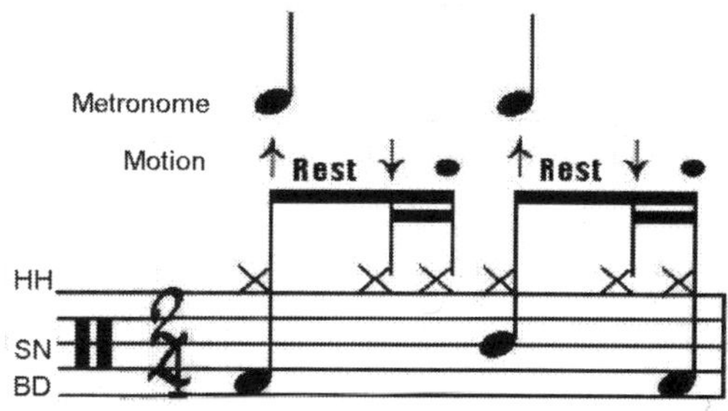

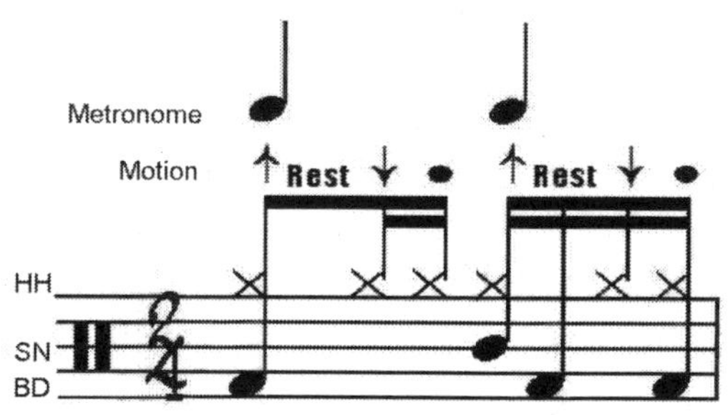

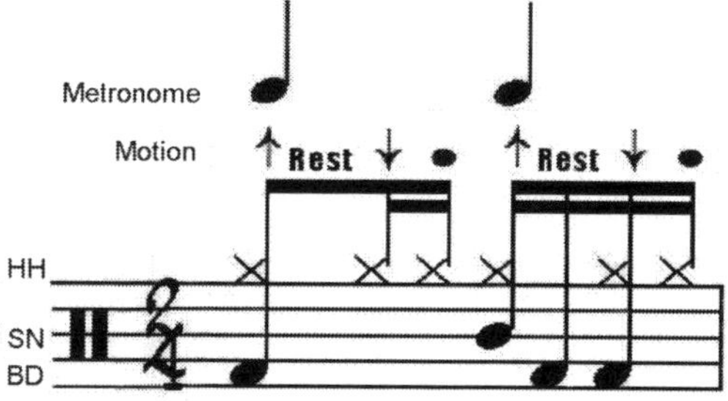

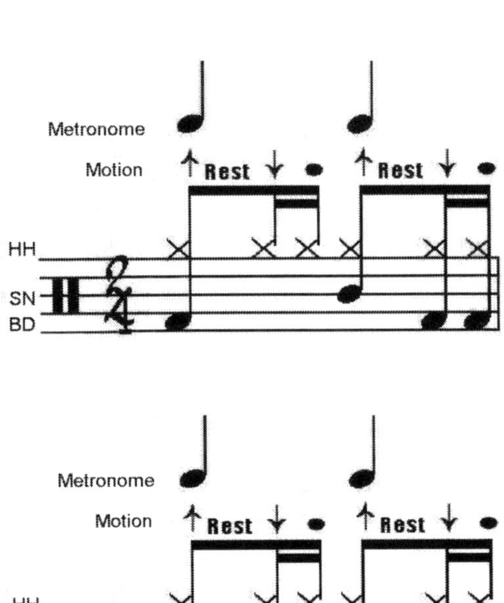
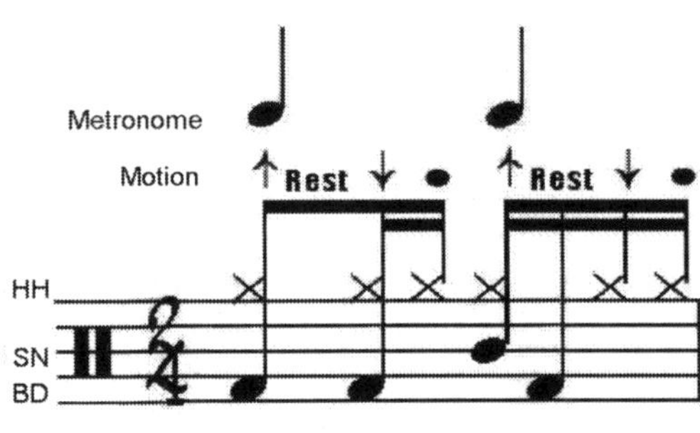
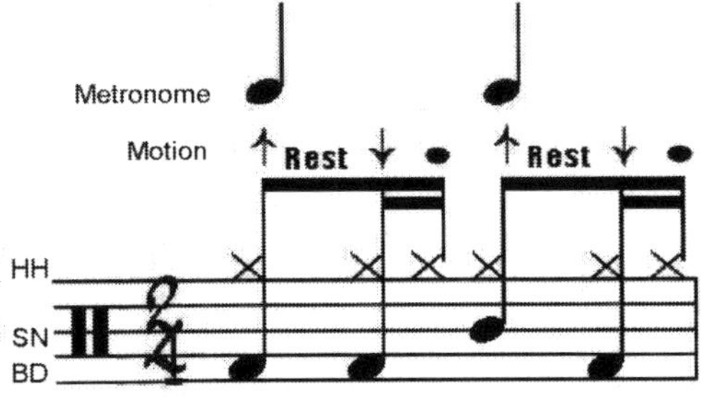
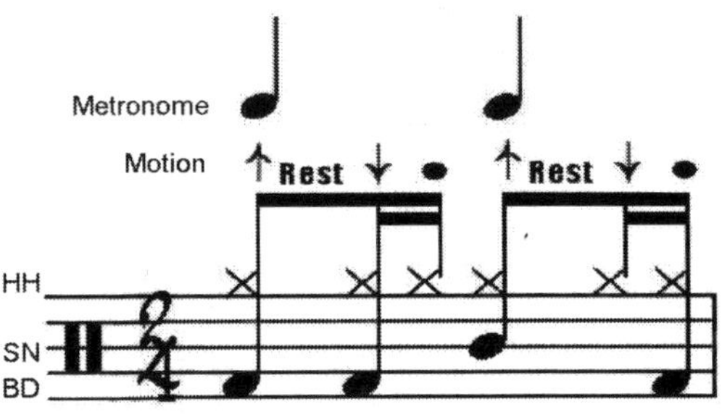
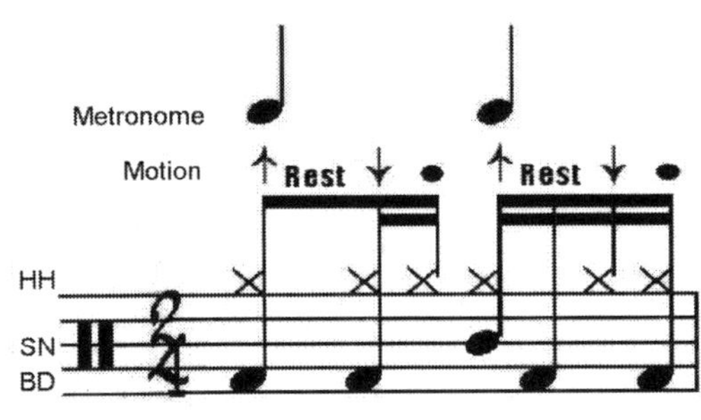
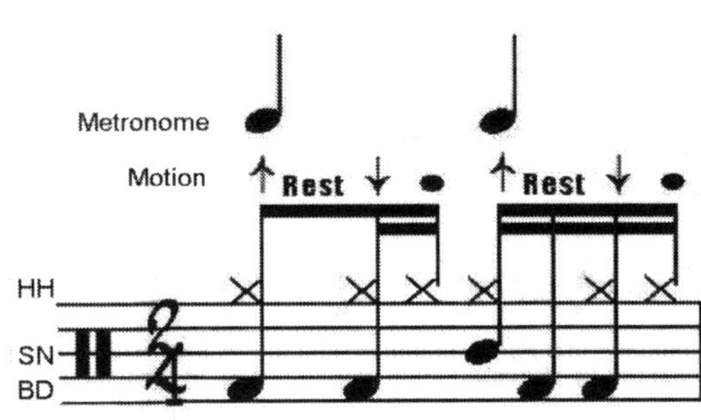
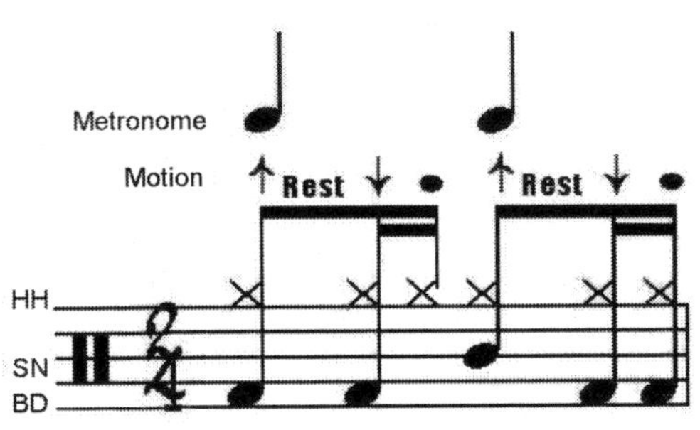
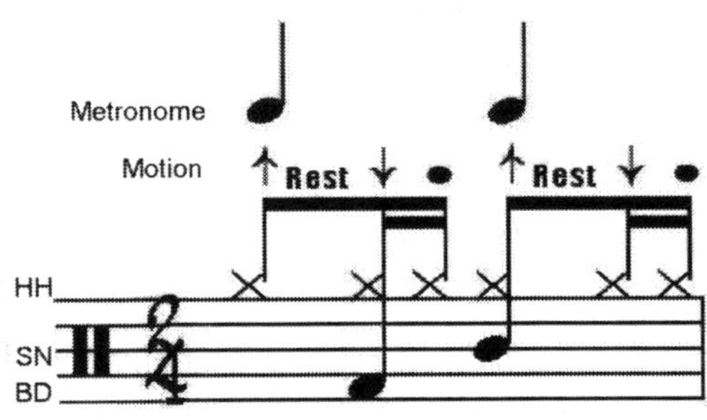

Metronome
Motion
Rest
HH
SN
BD

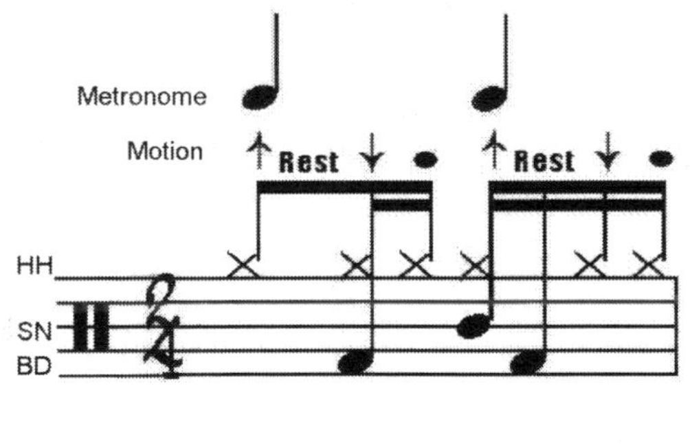

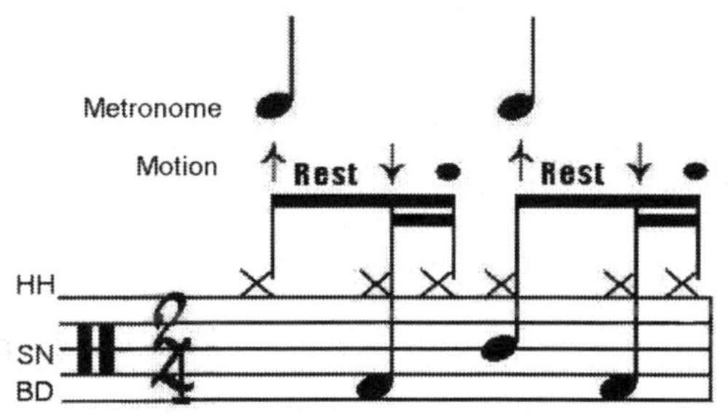

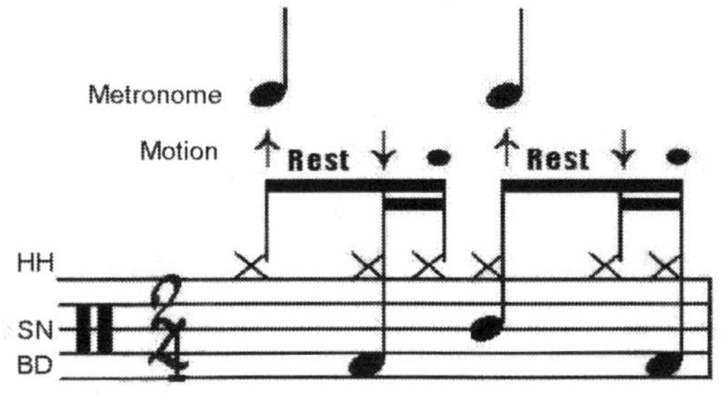

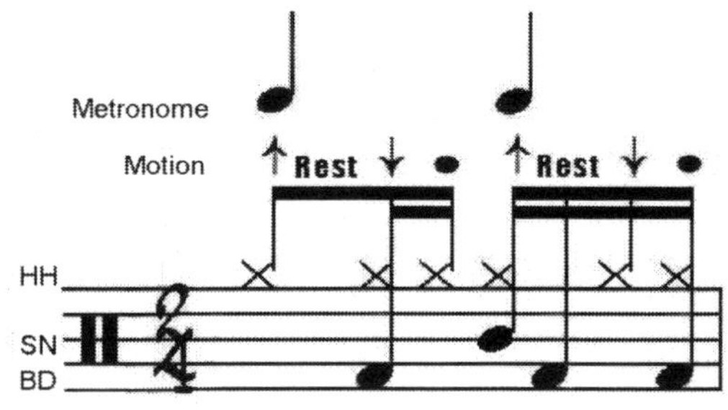

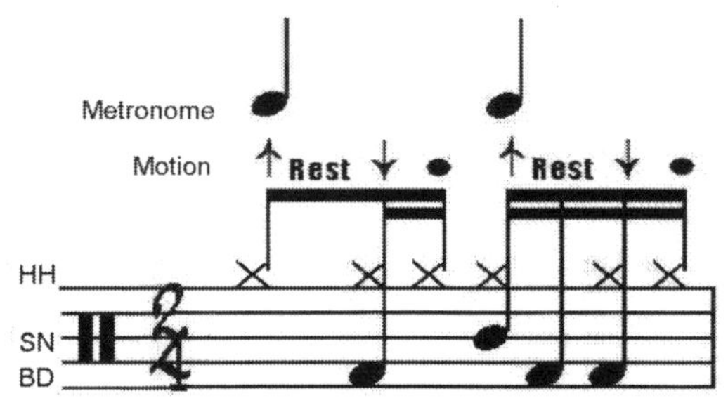

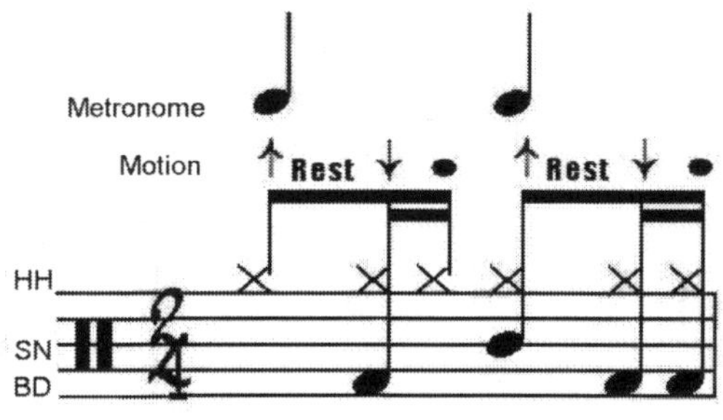

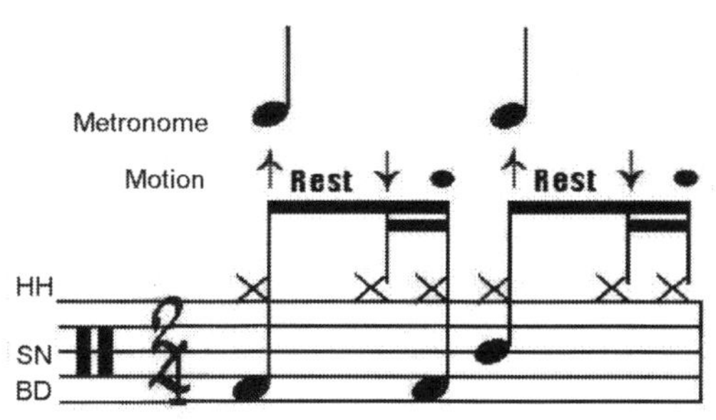

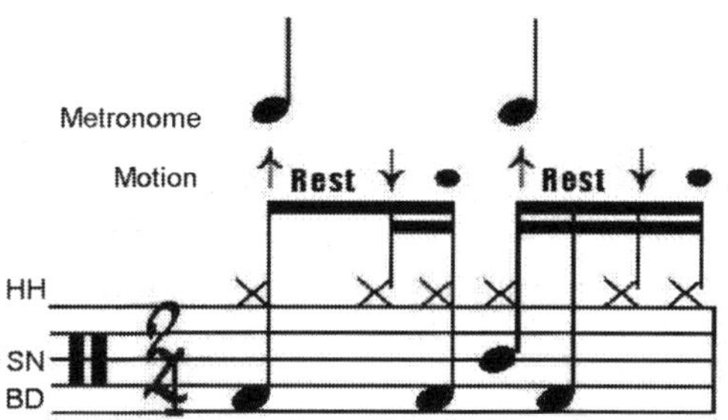

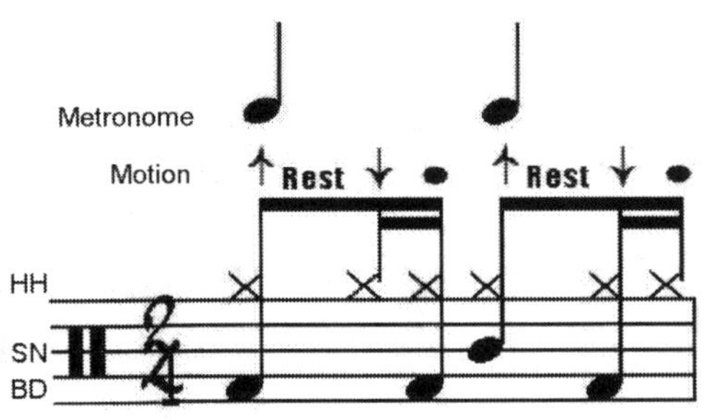

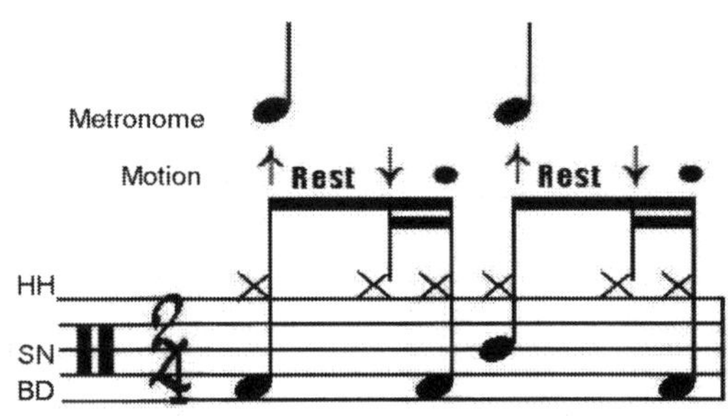

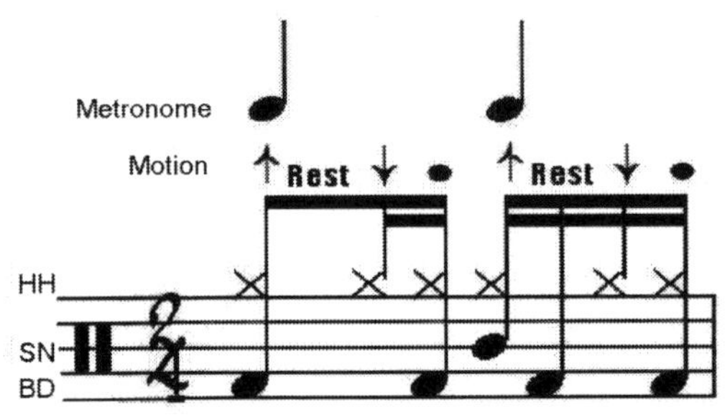

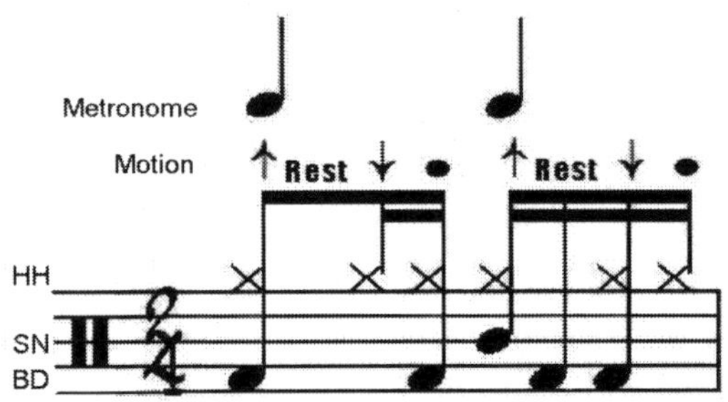

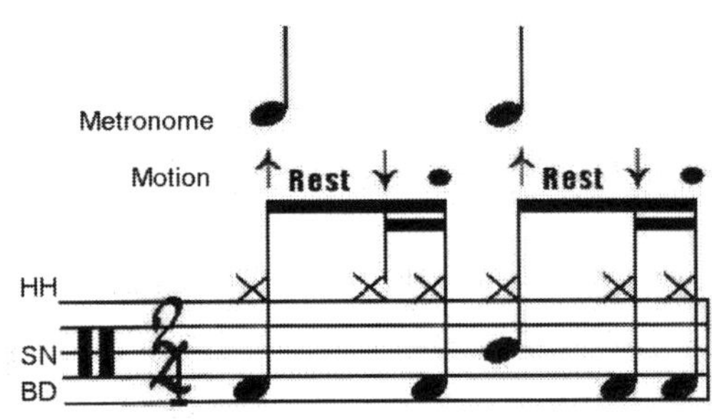

Basic Groove: Ghost Notes in the Snare Drum

In this section we'll be adding in Ghost Notes in the snare drum while continuing to move the BD around rhythmically.
First you need to know what a ghost note is; A Ghost Note is a snare drum note played lighter than a full stroke note. It's very similar to the accidental note on a Flam.
Follow the motions in the music and the Ghost Note will appear… No pun intended:

8th HH/ 16th Ghost/ BD variations

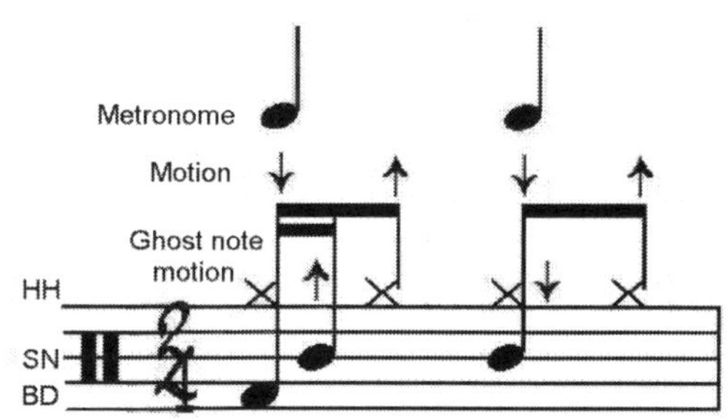

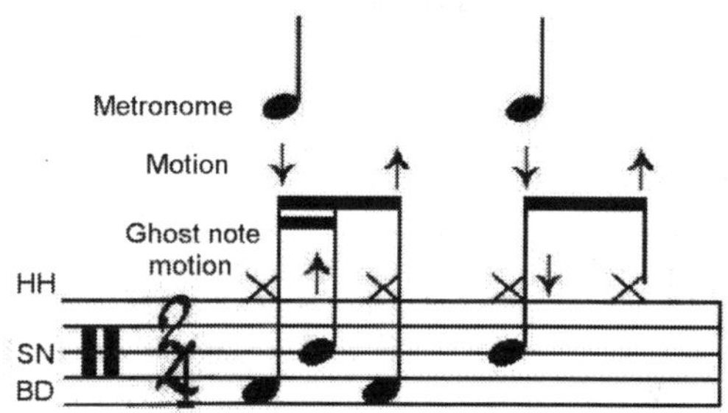

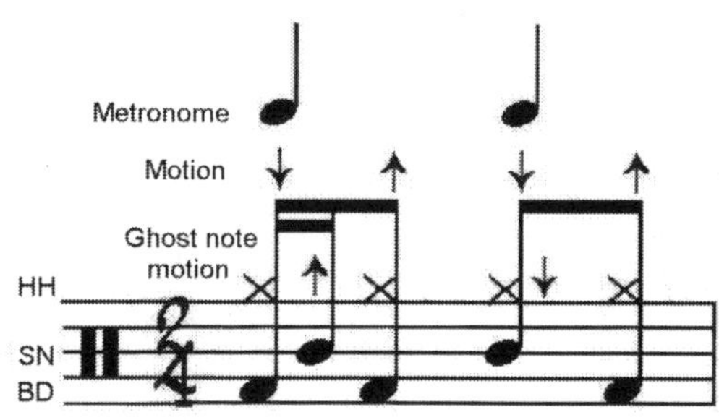

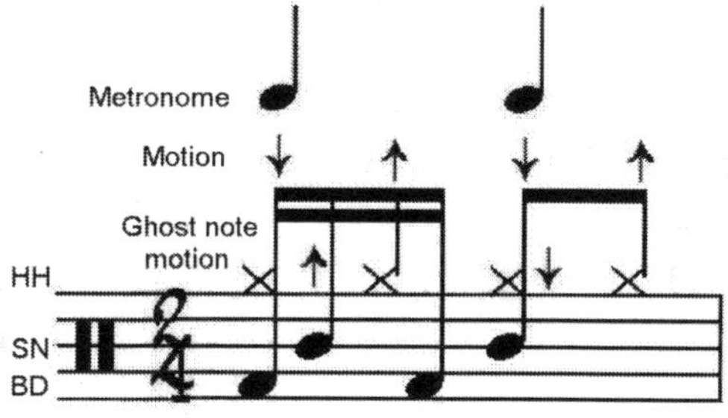

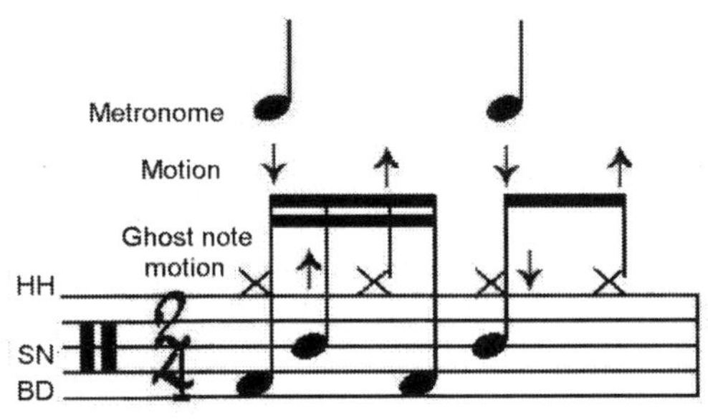
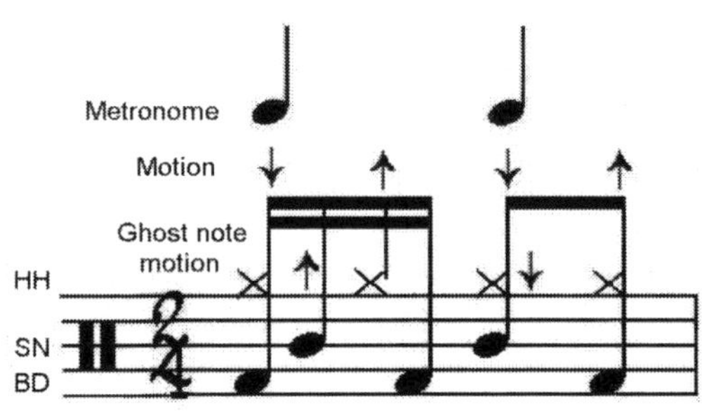
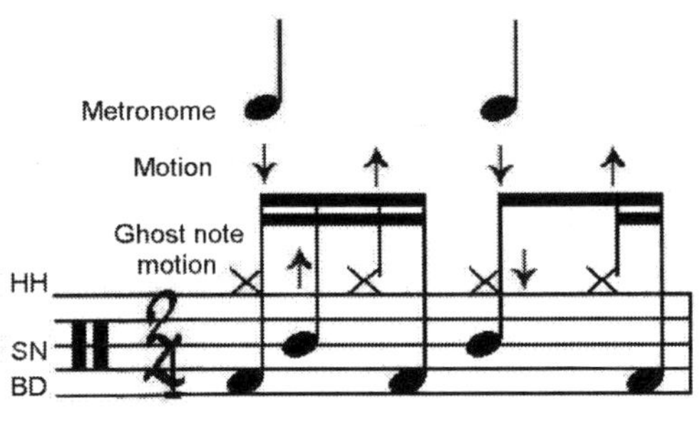
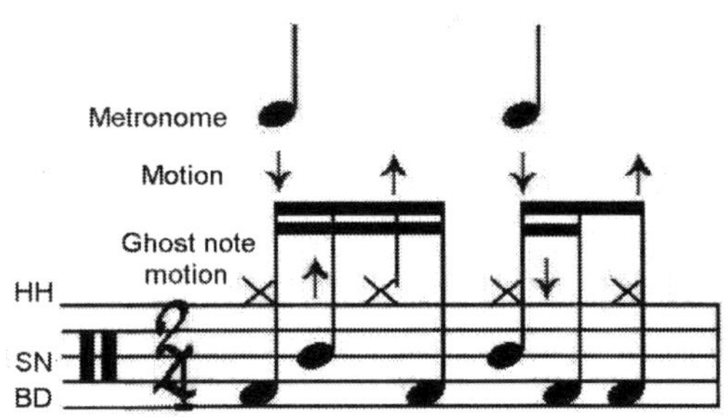
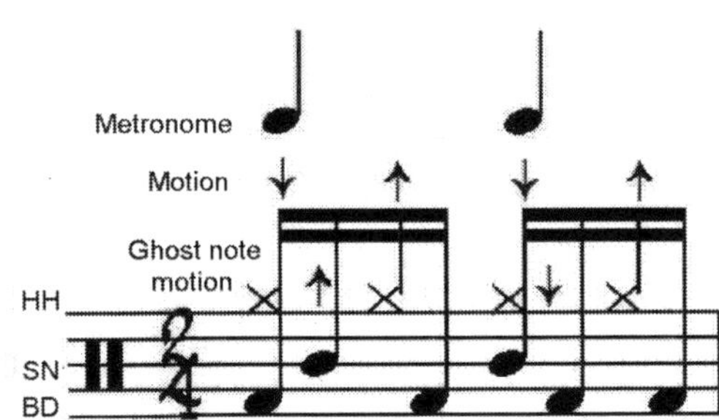

These next grooves add a 16th ghost note in the SN at the end of the phrase

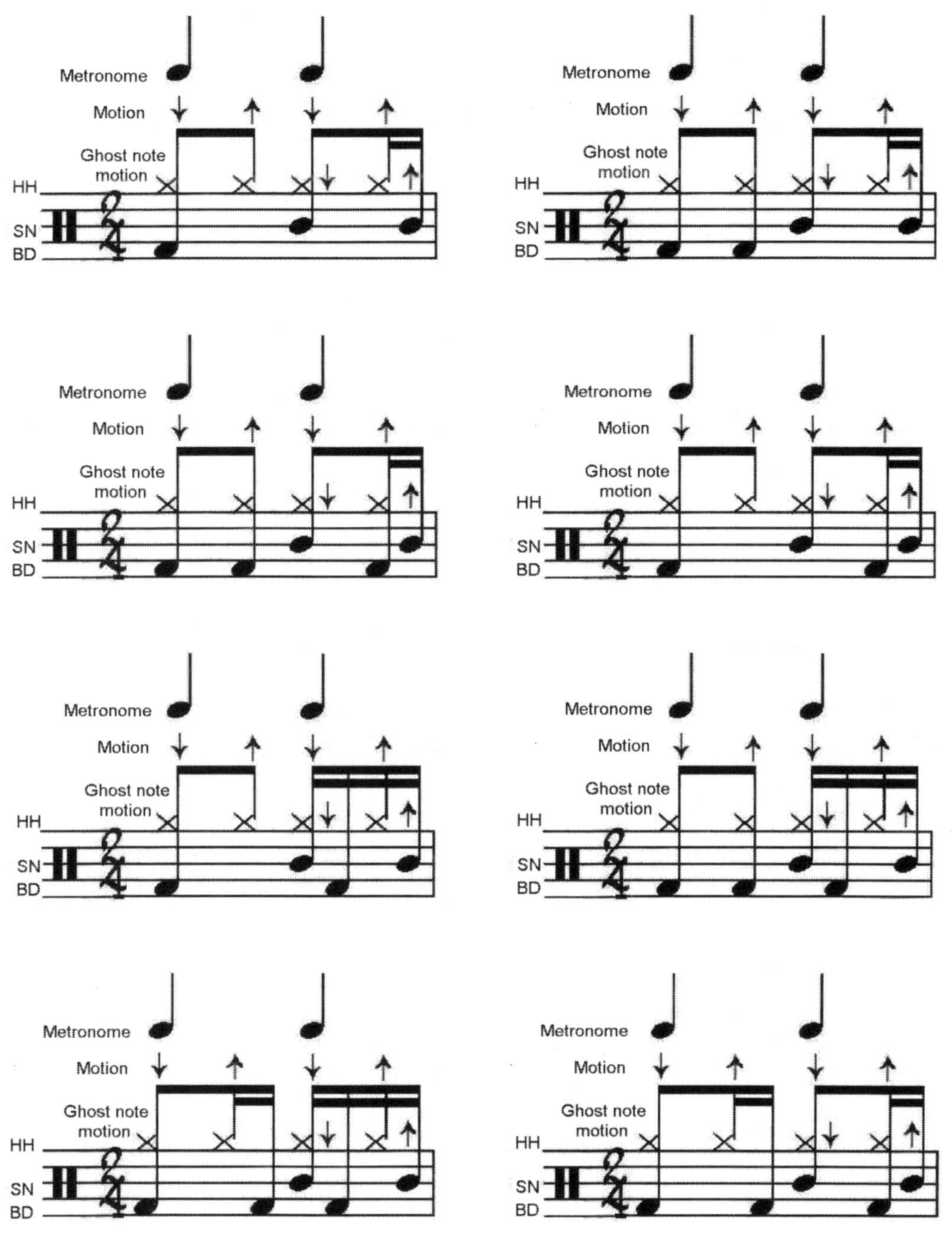

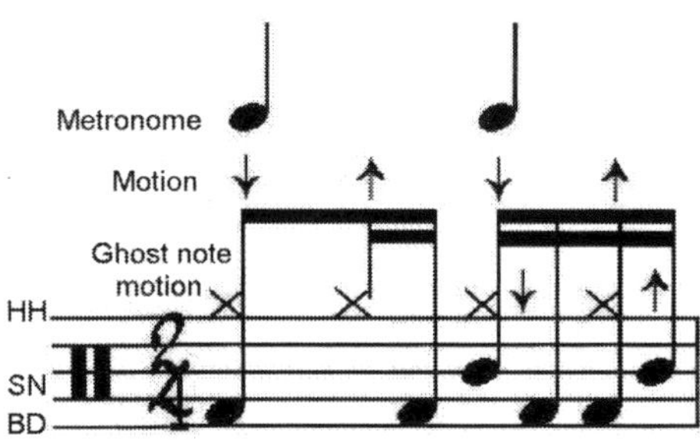

In the next grooves the SN hand will stay in the down position and playing a tap stroke then an up stroke to reset the accented down stroke. REMEMBER to follow the motions in the music:

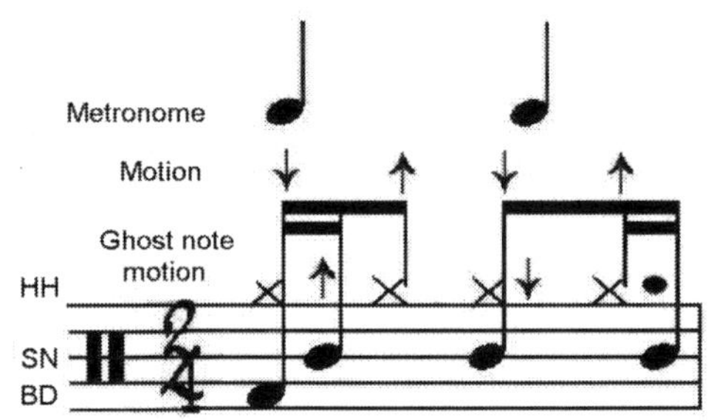 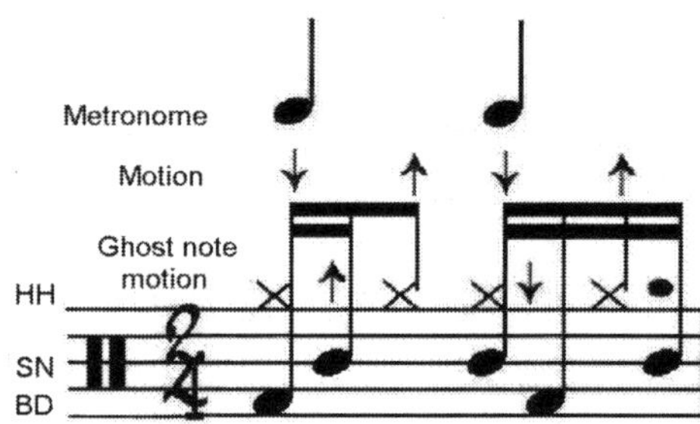

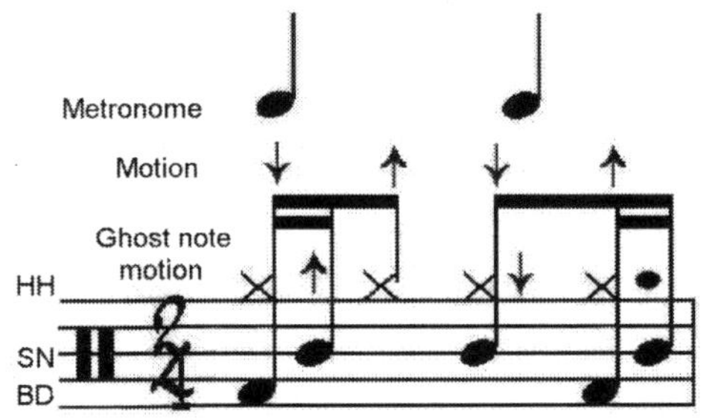 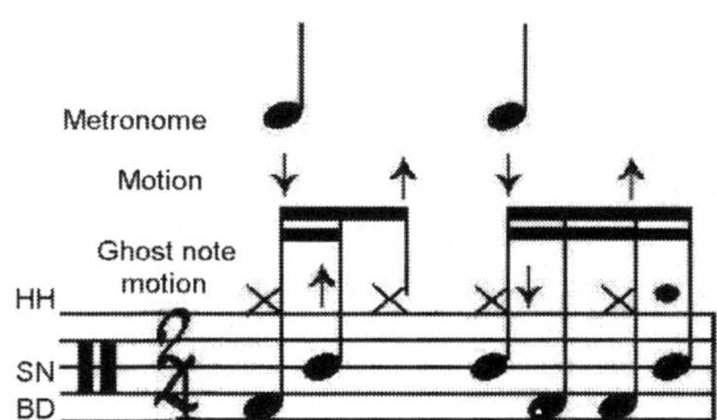

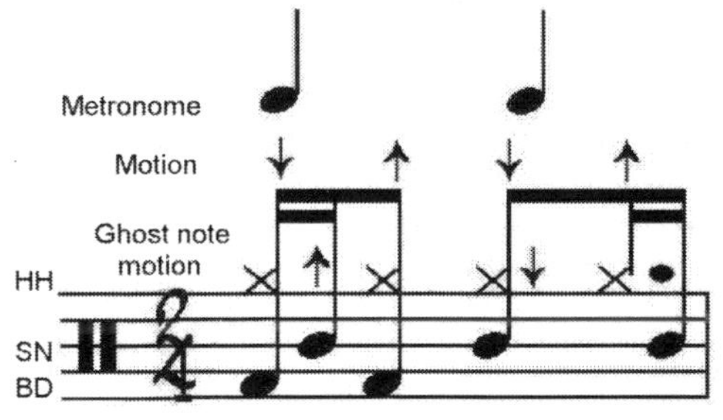

Metronome
Motion
Ghost note motion
HH
SN
BD

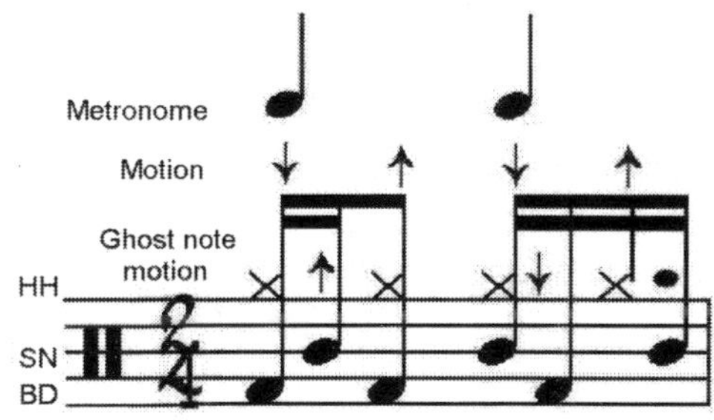

Metronome
Motion
Ghost note motion
HH
SN
BD

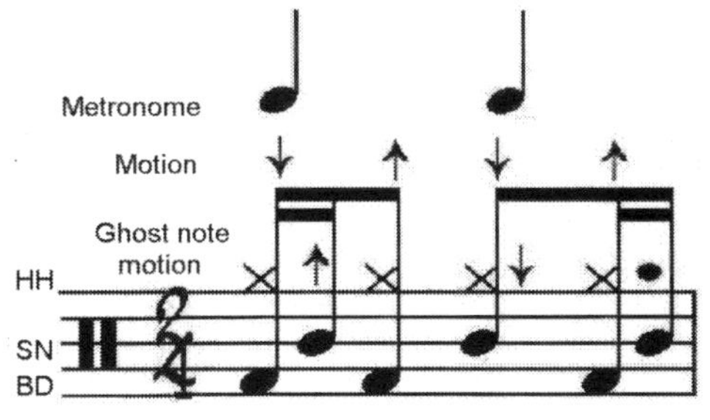

Metronome
Motion
Ghost note motion
HH
SN
BD

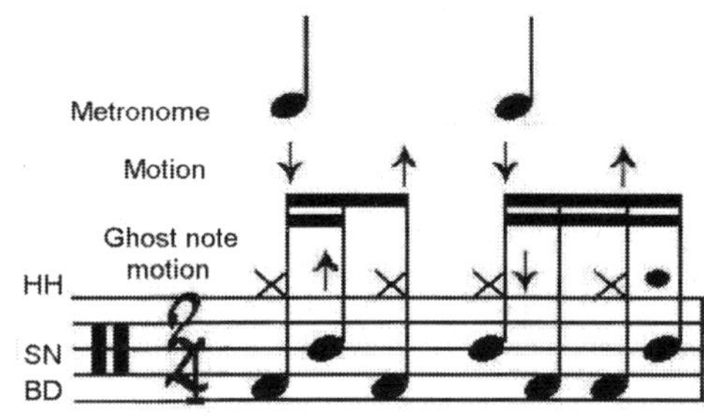

Metronome
Motion
Ghost note motion
HH
SN
BD

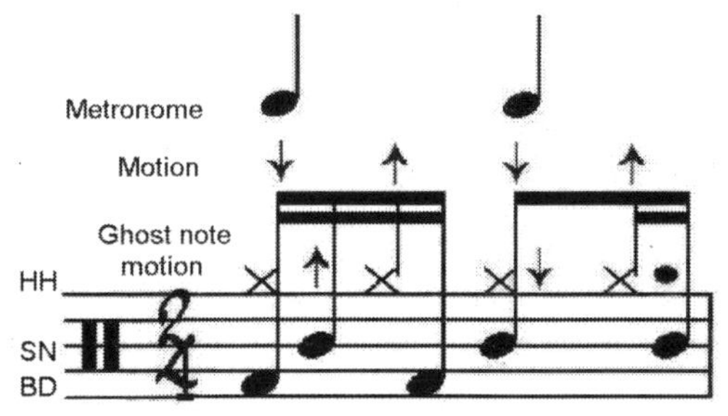

Metronome
Motion
Ghost note motion
HH
SN
BD

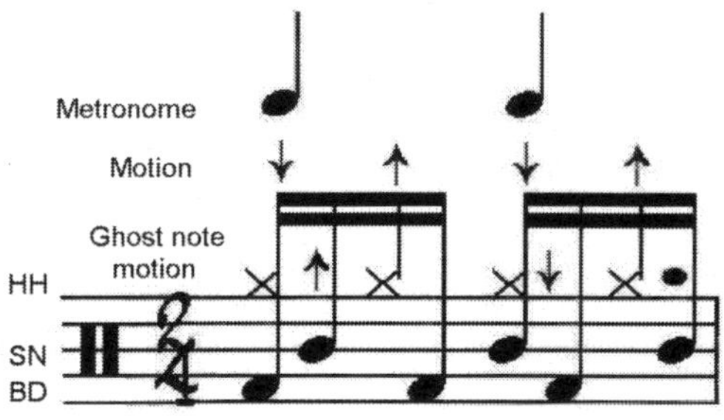

Metronome
Motion
Ghost note motion
HH
SN
BD

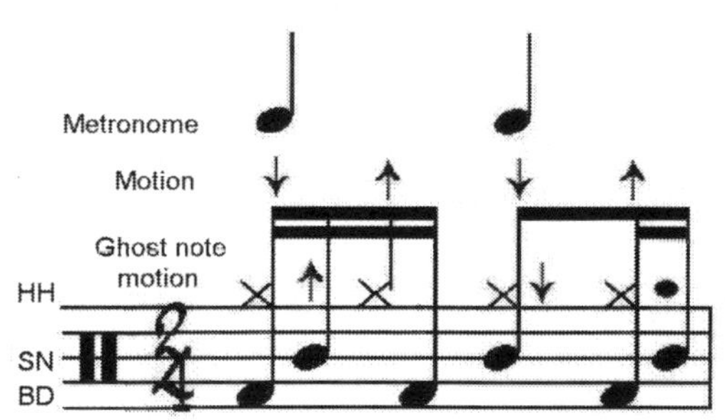

Metronome
Motion
Ghost note motion
HH
SN
BD

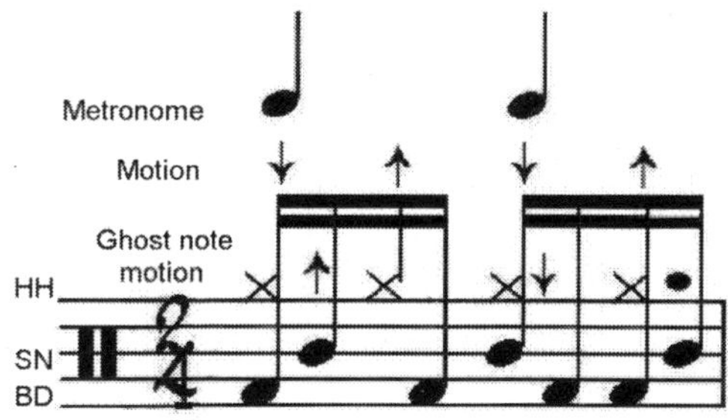

Metronome
Motion
Ghost note motion
HH
SN
BD

The final 16th ghost SN groove will add a double to the 2nd beat

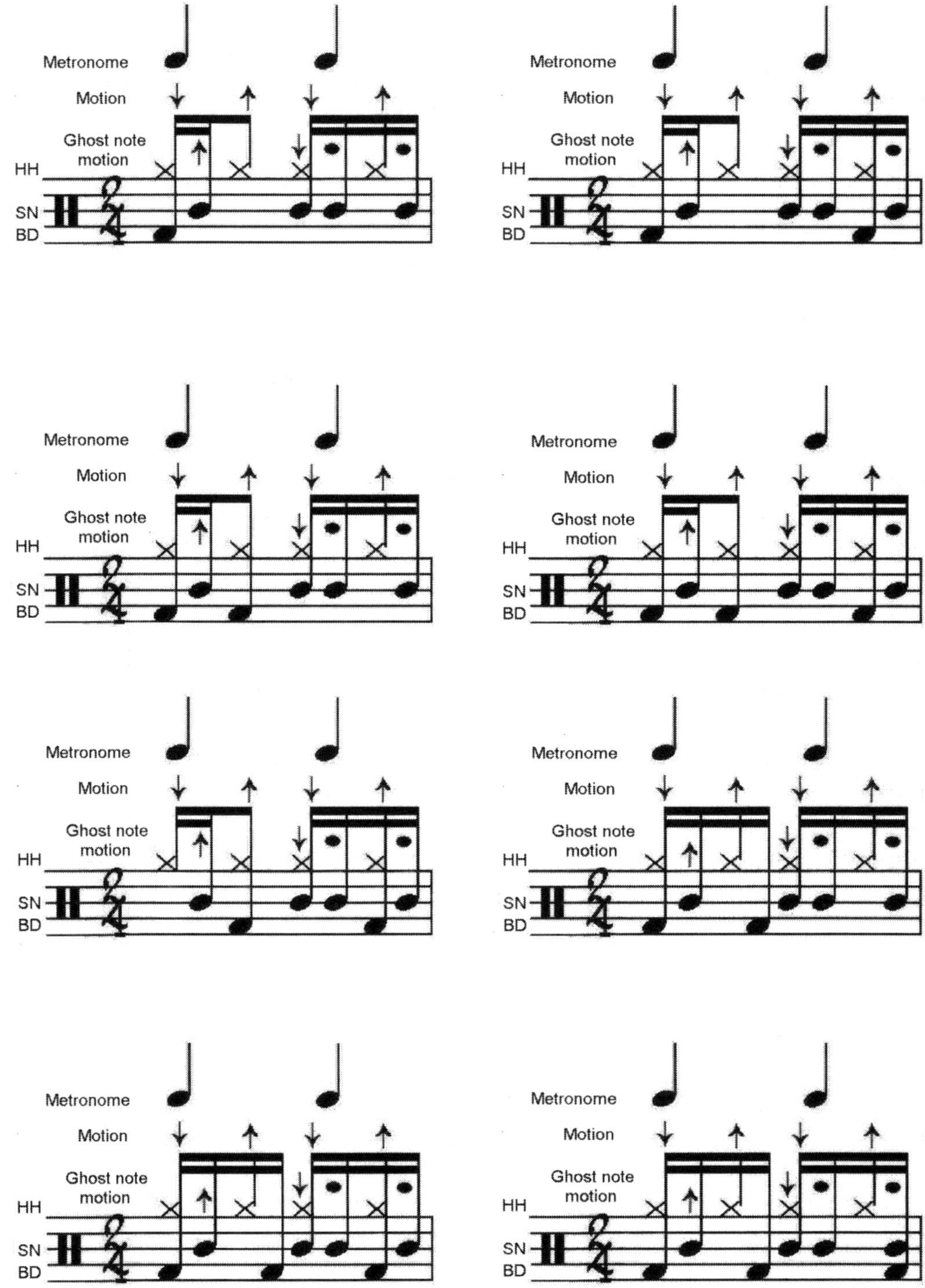

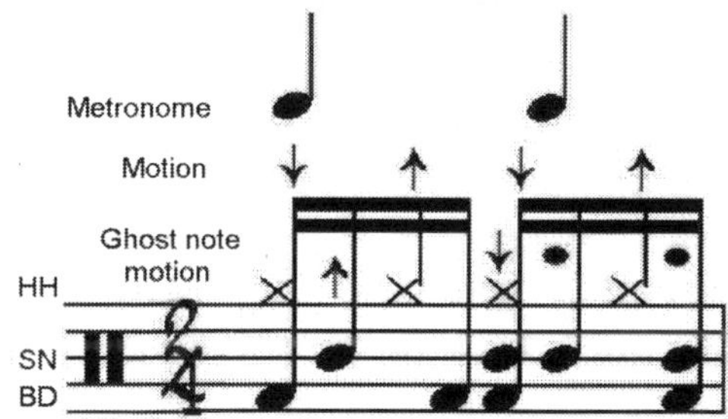

Basic Groove: 3 Note 16ths in HH/ Ghost Notes/ BD Variations

Follow the motions on the music to help with grooving and coordination:

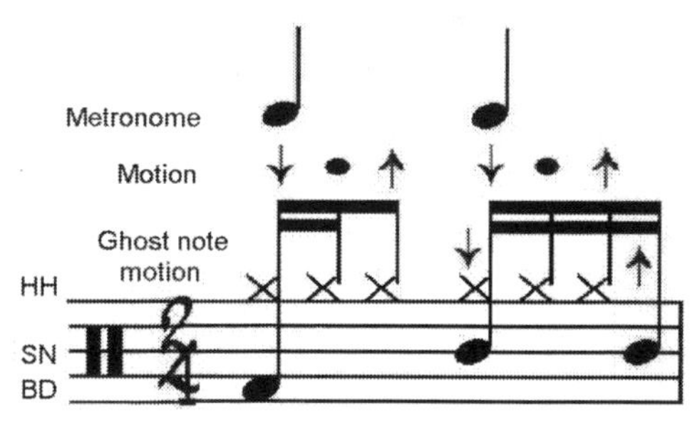

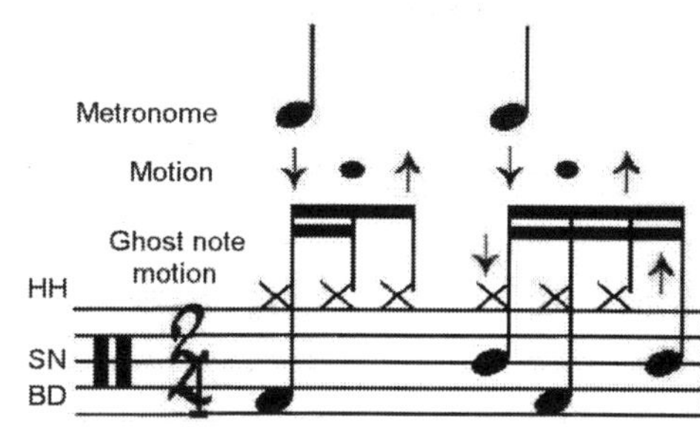

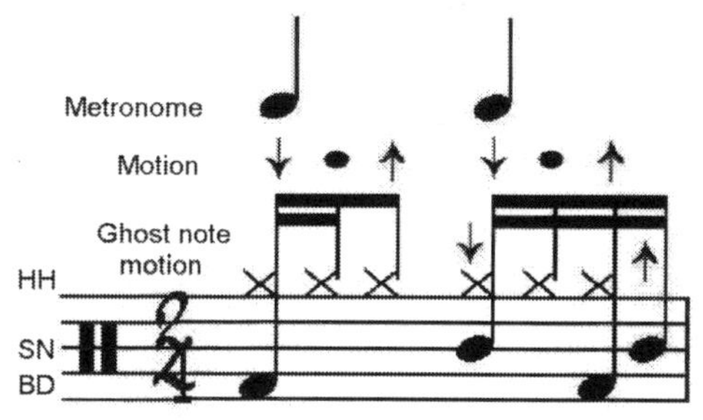

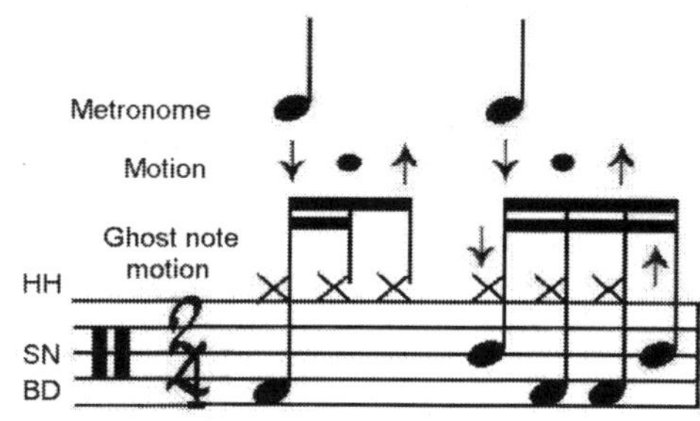

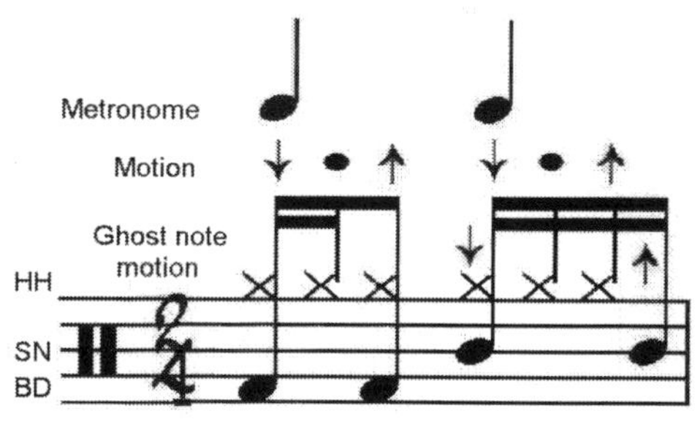

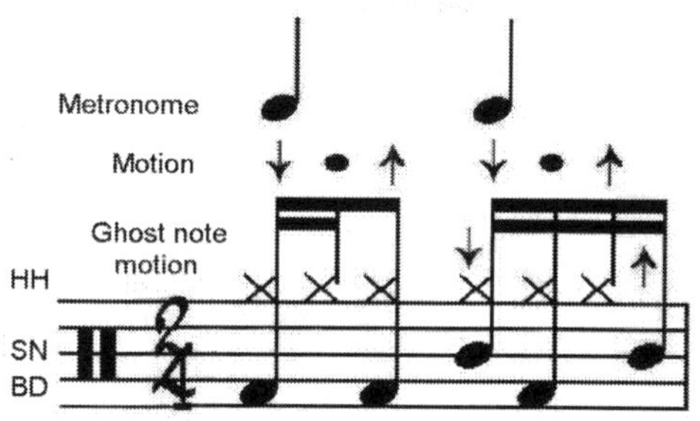

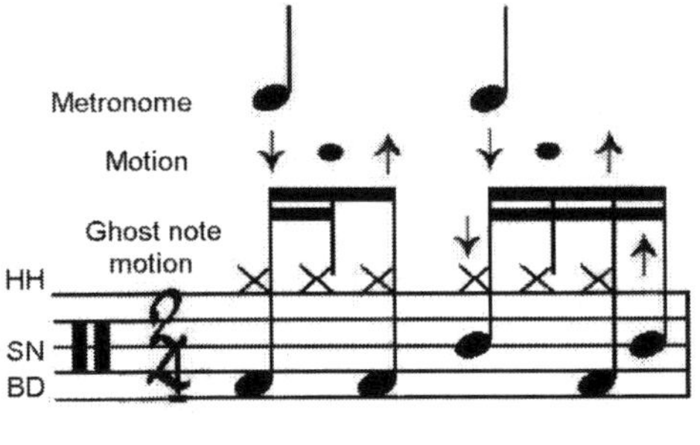

Metronome
Motion
Ghost note motion
HH
SN
BD

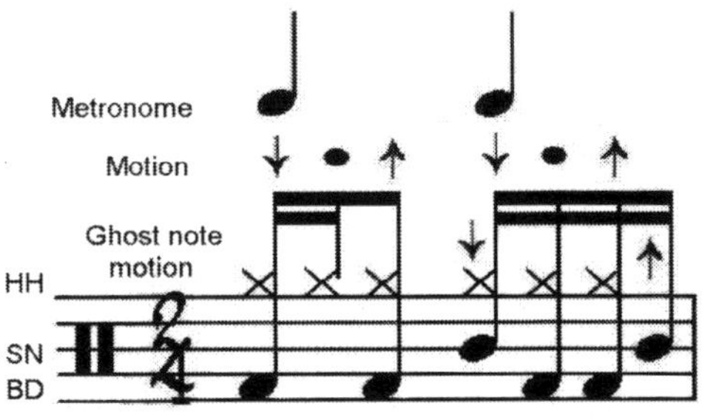

Metronome
Motion
Ghost note motion
HH
SN
BD

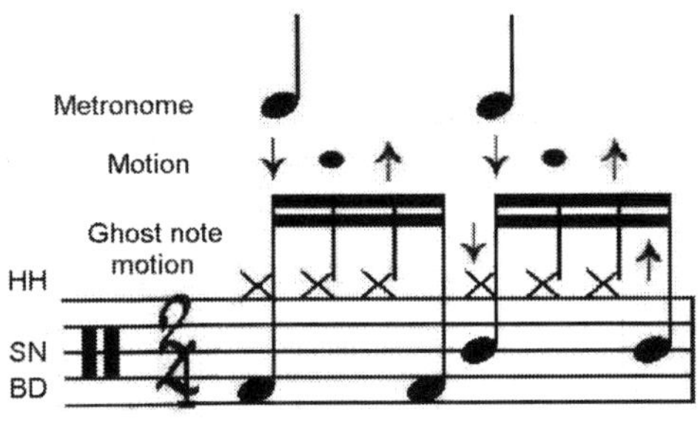

Metronome
Motion
Ghost note motion
HH
SN
BD

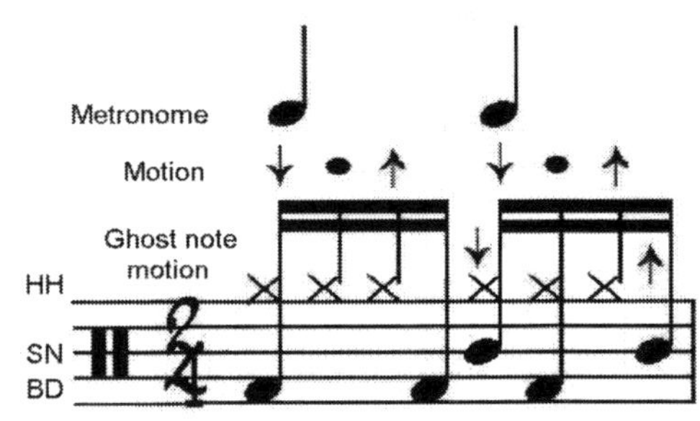

Metronome
Motion
Ghost note motion
HH
SN
BD

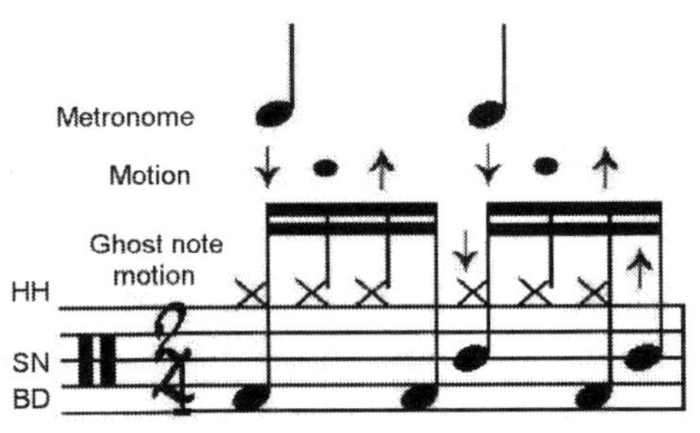

Metronome
Motion
Ghost note motion
HH
SN
BD

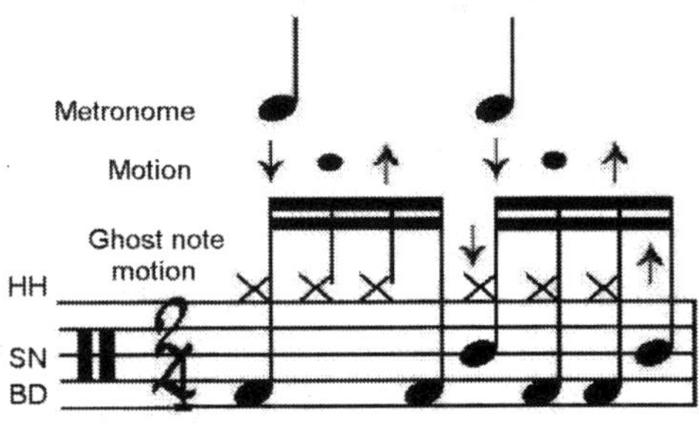

Metronome
Motion
Ghost note motion
HH
SN
BD

Add ghost notes to the middle of this 16th note pattern

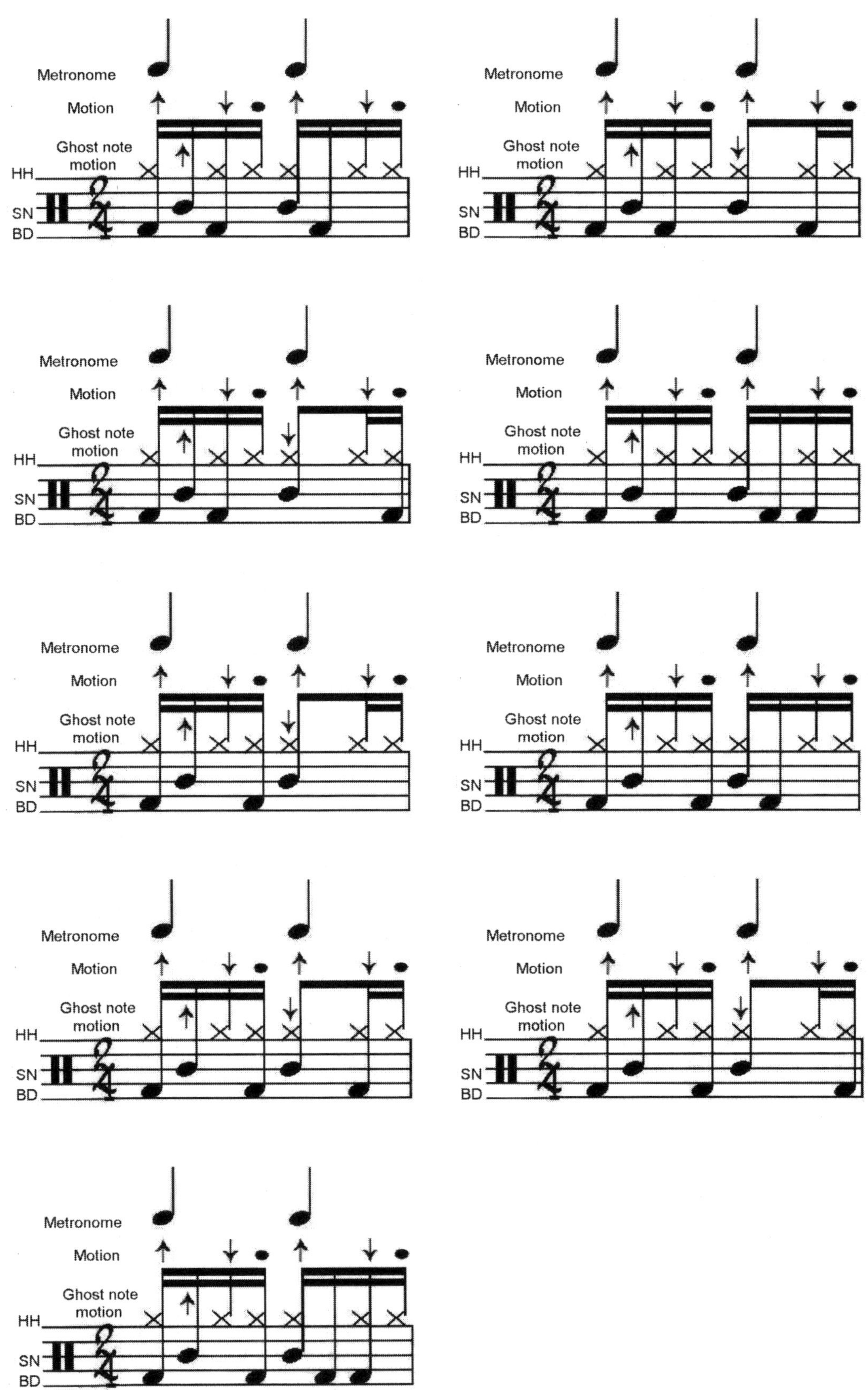

Basic Groove: Shuffle Ghost Notes

 With these Ghost Notes the rhythm will be the same as the HH. Basically the SN hand is filling in the Triplet feel:

Chapter Summary

Now that you've got all these grooves mix and match to make interesting rhythmical phrases. Take grooves from Chapter 1 and mix them with ghost note grooves the possibilities are endless. This summary should be a lifelong journey in creativity… Explore!

Chapter 3

Basic Motion: Down/Bounce/Bounce/Up

The final stroke theory uses 2 bounces to make the 4-note grouping. This is an advanced grouping that uses lots of control of the stick. The only rudiment that we're going to study in this book that uses it is the Flam Paradiddle. While you're learning it you'll try the advanced 4 Stroke Roll and 4 note buzzing technique. But first the breakdown:

Hit the drum let the stick rebound

Next let it bounce and rebound for 2 notes while the hand stays stationary

The last stroke (up)when the arm/wrist is resetting

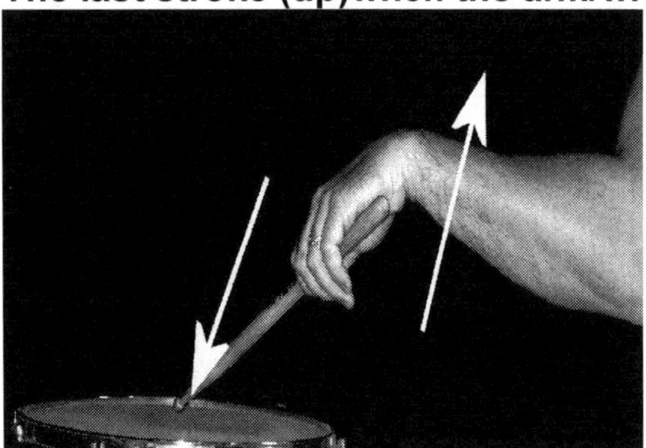

4 Stroke Exercise:

Here's the way the motions look musically Practice this exercise to the metronome and make it flow evenly. Then switch to the LH.

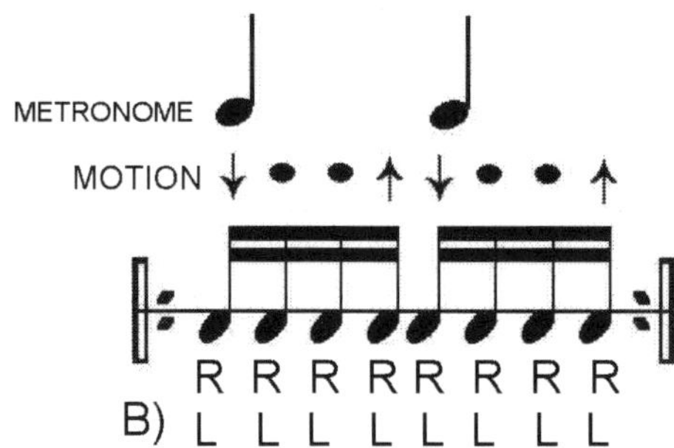

The Four Stroke Roll and Buzzing:

These exercises will expand your stick control and buzz control. Practice carefully and slowly and remember not to force the strokes, loose hands. Practice the buzz strokes first then move on to the 4 stroke roll.

4 Buzz   **Alternating 4 Stroke Roll**

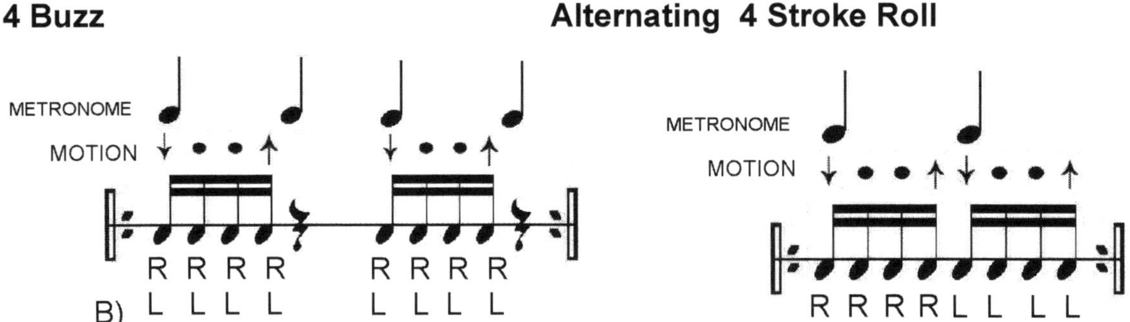

Rudiment Study

The Flam Paradiddle

On the third note of the grouping starts the 4 stroke pattern. Practice this exercise slowly and don't force the 4 notes let them flow.

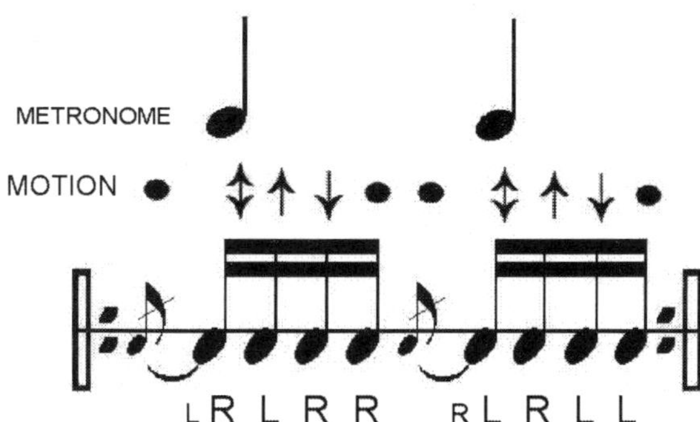

Exercise 6: 4 Stroke Alternating Roll into Flam Paradiddle

This hybrid rudiment uses the 4 stroke roll and the flam paradiddle to help with the bounce stroke. Play this slowly and cafully study the movement to help accomplish the coordination.

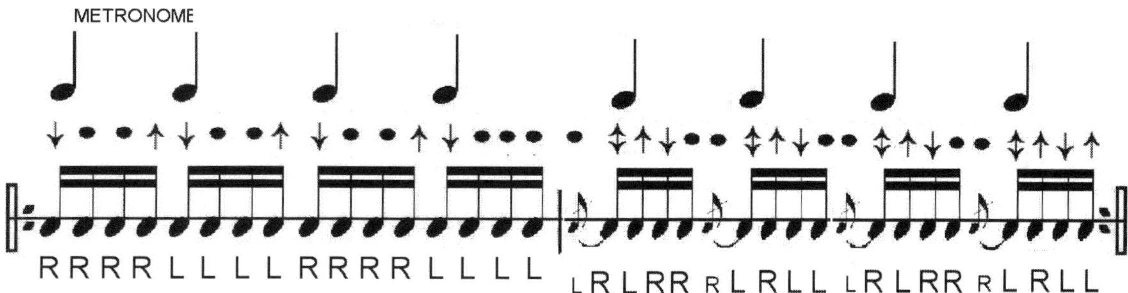

Syncopations and the Art of Building a Fill

Drum fills are an expression of the music on the drums. If we were to play groove all the time it would sound monotonous. Even dance songs, which are ALL about the groove, have some sort of syncopated rhythmical device to break it up. On the flip side too many fills disrupts the flow of the music and makes it undesireable. As an example, if you were to play all 16th notes un-orchestrated as a fill over two measures it would eventually sound something like this:
implayningadrumfillthats16thnotesthatlaststtwomeasuresormore
Hard to read but if you add breaks and punctuation to the sentence the point becomes clearer. The pauses let you reflect on what you've heard and give you a chance to decide on your response. Music especially drums needs breaks and punctuation to make it clear and get the point across.
In this lesson we'll take a well know syncopated rhythm and use that as a guide for inspiration on the drums. By adding rudiments and conceptual ideas the syncopated rhythm will jump to life on the set.

Syncopated Listening:

Let's make a fill from the syncopation of "Kashmir" from Led Zeppelin. The drums play a solid backbeat and the vocals are long stretched out phrases. The Da Da Da rhythm of the guitar and bass is the major syncopation in the song and counterbalances the simplicity of the other instruments. Technically it's a 12 beat long syncopation, which is a rhythmical take on a standard blues form.

Looking like this:

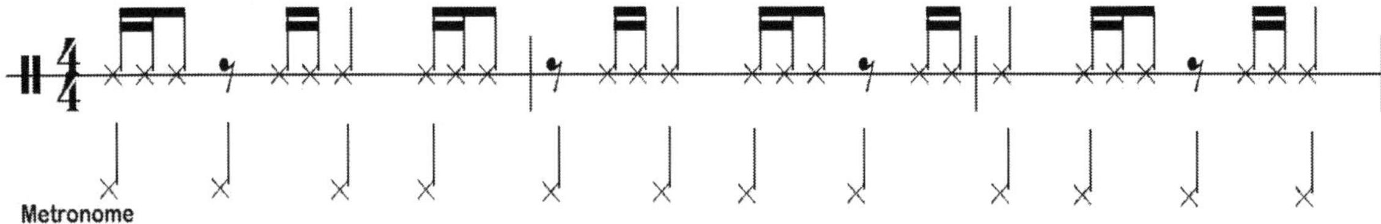

To use this as a fill rhythm let's use the first measure of the phrase:

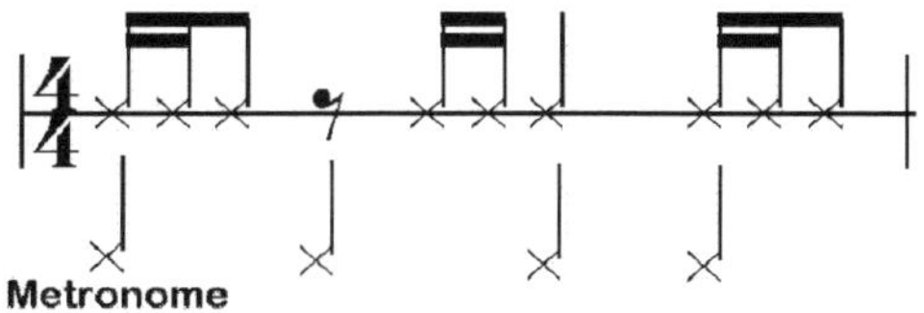

Now take measures 2 and 3 start the process over:

Measure 2:

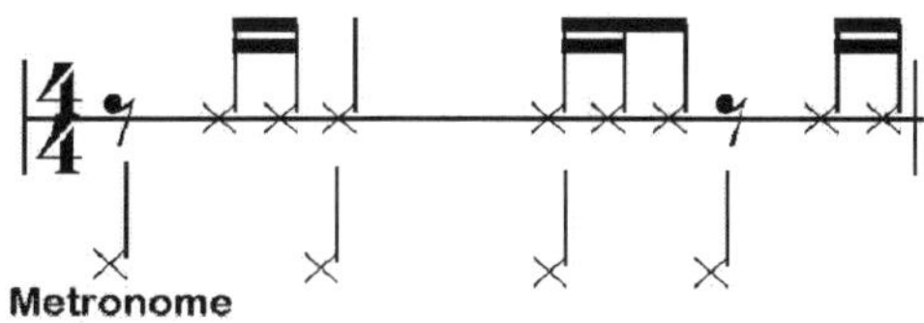

Measure 3:

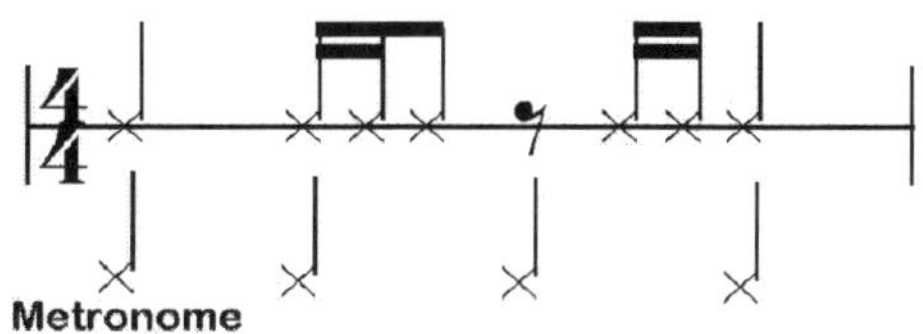

Exercise 7: The 6 Stroke Roll

The 6 stroke roll is from The Swiss Rudiments. It played two doubles and two singles. The double strokes are twice the speed of the singles.

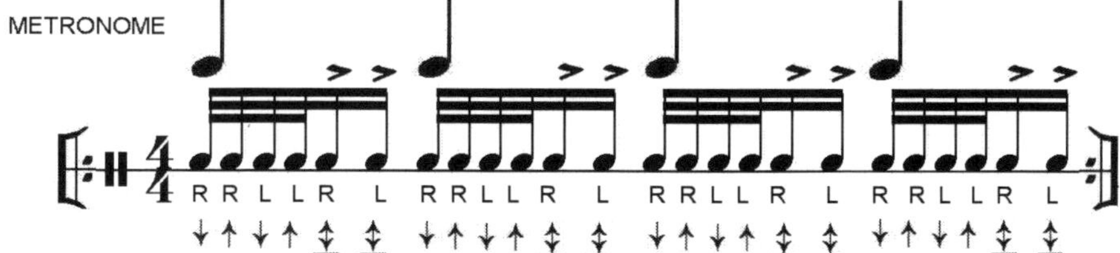

Using The 6 Stroke Roll in Syncopation:

Using the same syncopation we'll now use the 6 Stroke Roll to accentuate the syncopation.

As we did before, isolate the first measure of the phrase:

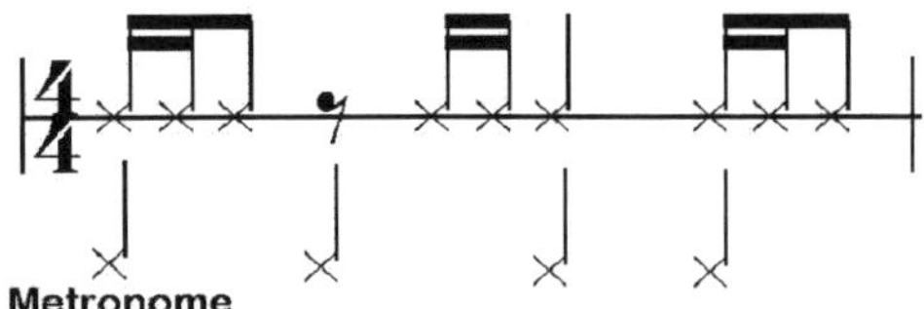

Now we'll use it in the syncopation. Remember to sing and feel the quarter note go by:

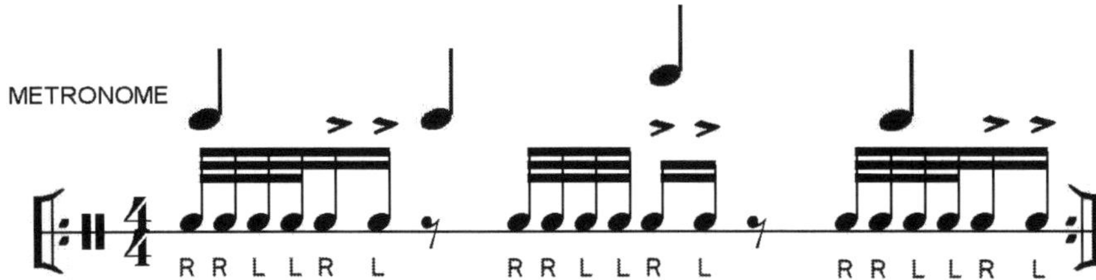

In this exercise you'll add the remaining 16th notes in the rests and repeat it to help with your double stroke and single stroke switching we'll break down the syncopations into 3 separate exercises. Repeat until solid then switch to a LH start:

1)

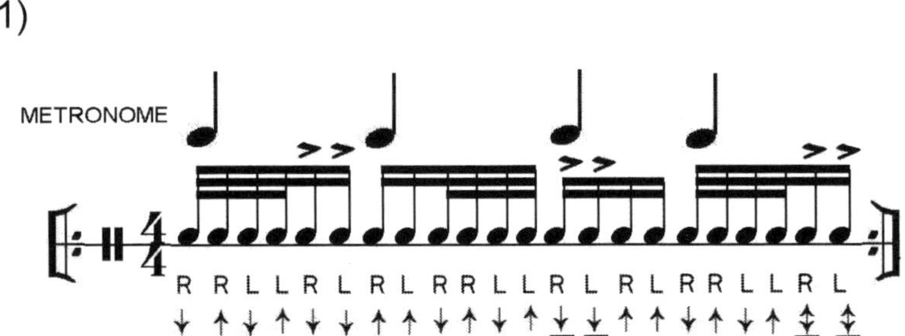

2)

3)

Practice the sticking exercises on a practice pad with a metronome to get the feel and coordination down. Use the motion to move your hands around the drum set. Here's exercise 1 using a typical orchestration. Take all the exercises and move them around using the same theory:

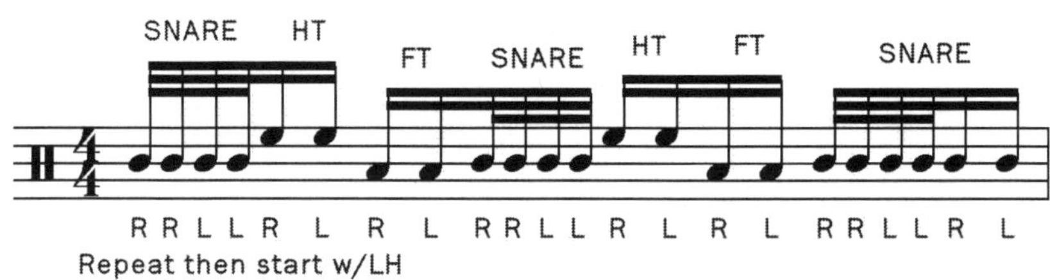

The Linear 6 Stroke Roll

This concept will be fully orchestrated for you. That doesn't mean you should learn these and move on. Mess around with the idea on the drums you'll definately find one that sounds really cool

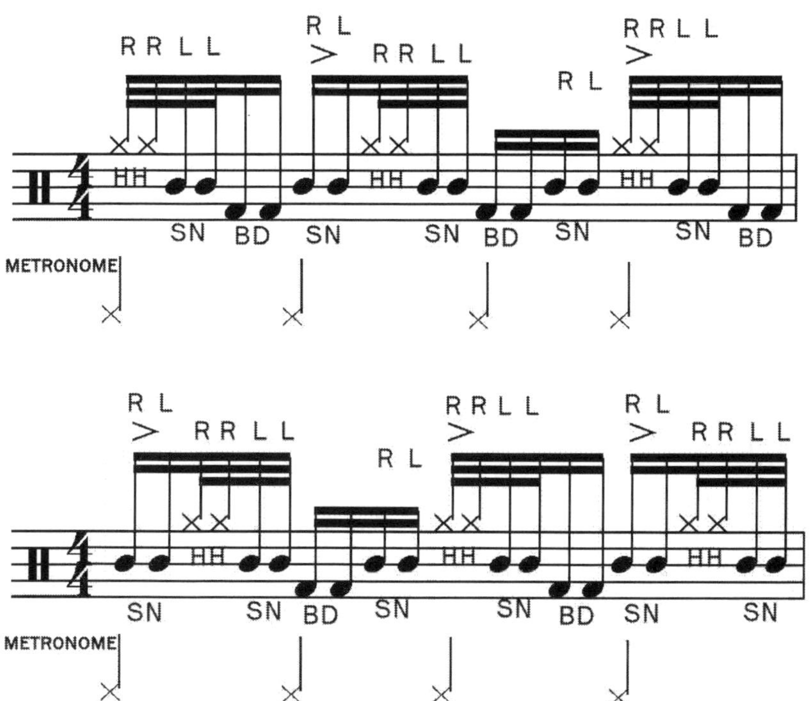

As you can see a wealth of fill ideas and grooves can be pulled out of a simple syncopation from a catchy melody. Find other cool syncopated patterns in the melodies of songs you listen to and apply these techniques to expand your rhythmical vocabulary. Here's some additional ideas.

Exercise 7: The Ruff

Let's start with a rudiment called The Ruff. It's played with 2 grace notes and then a final stroke. Like The Flam, the grace notes have no rhythmic value so the last note will lock in with the metronome. Play a. first until comfortable then switch to the opposite hand lead:

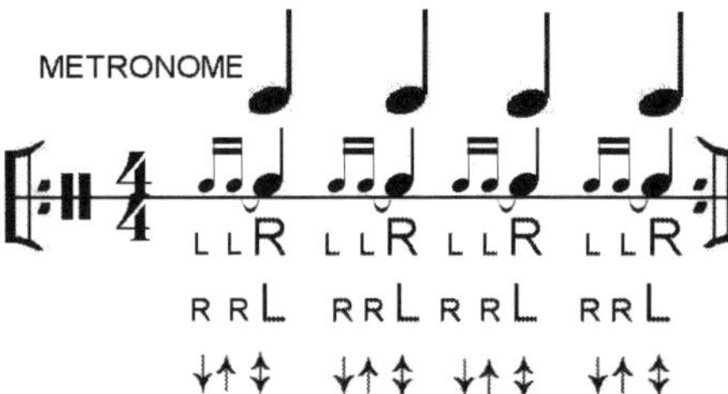

Here's The Ruff applied to the 3 syncopated rhythms. After you get comfortable with the RH lead switch over to the LH lead for more exercises:

1)

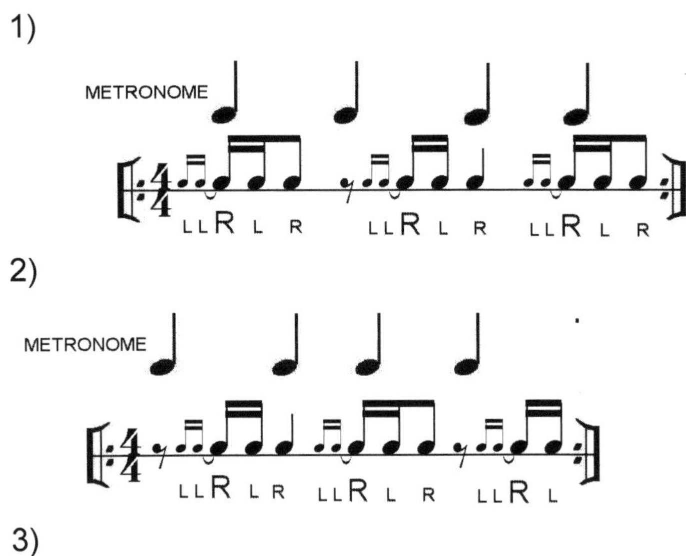

2)

3)

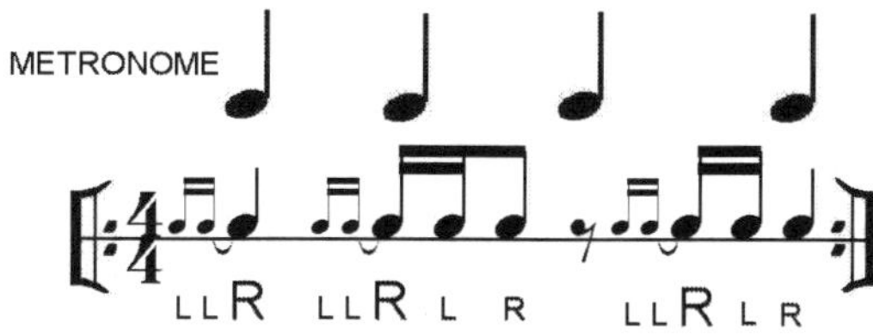

As with the 6 stroke roll we'll compose it rhythmically around the drum set:

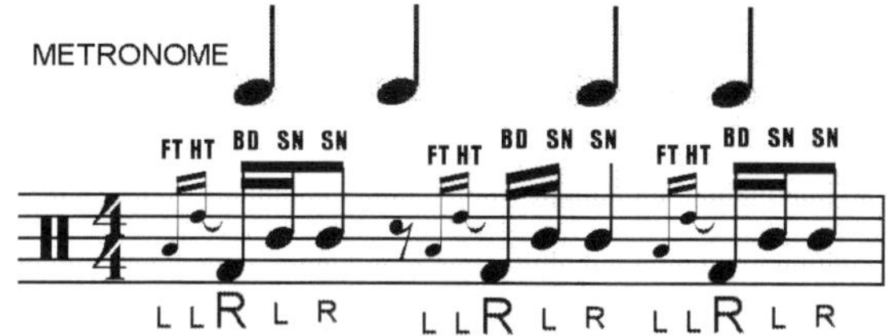

Adding The Flam to Syncopation

As you've learnt earlier, The flam is another accidental rudiment. The grace note again has no rhythmic value and has a line drawn through it for that reason. Play the 3 examples as written. When comfortable switch starting hands.

1)

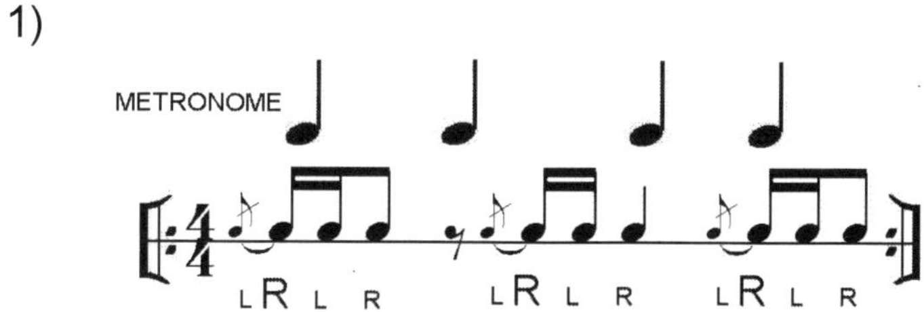

2)

3)

The 26 Standard American Rudiments

In the last sections we've taken some of the rudiments and used them as examples of where you'd find the basic motions. Here are the 26 Standard American Rudiment in order. Pay attention to the motions they'll help with the speed and flow:

#1 The Single Stroke Roll

As I said before the most important rudiment you'll ever need to know. You're going to start with 2 down Strokes then 2 Up Strokes then repeat. Start with your R.H. first then stop and do a L.H. lead.

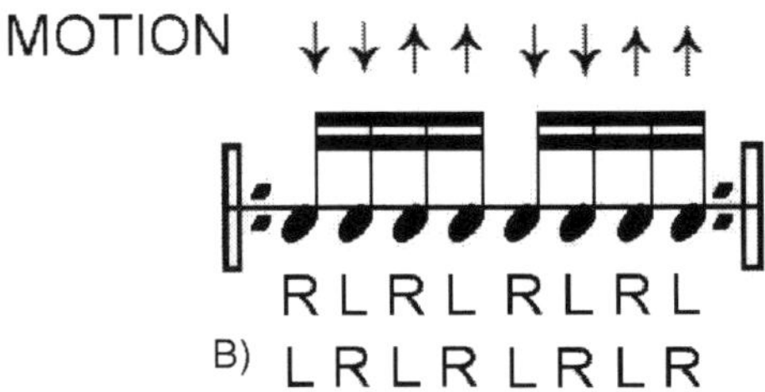

#2 The Double Stroke Roll

The second most commonly used rudiment. Playing it open you'll have the fulcrum loose, when you switch to buzz that fulcrum squeezes and releases. If you have problems with the Buzz roll restudy the multiple bounce section of the book:

Open roll: **Buzz roll:**

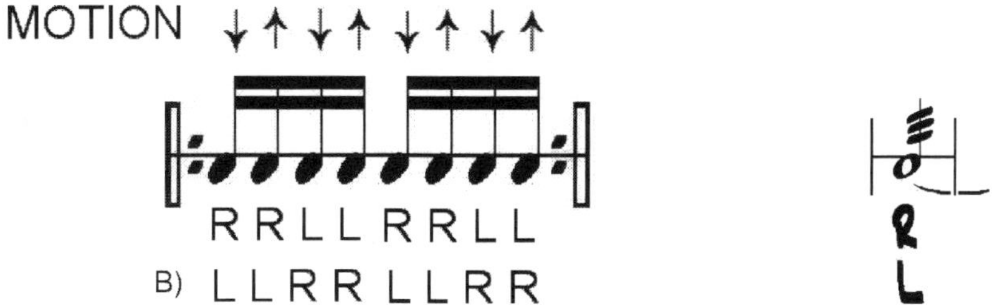

#3 The 5 Stroke Roll

This is the start of the roll section. I've written them open but of course they all have a buzz version as well. To perform the Buzz squeeze the fulcrum on the DOWN stroke and release on the UP.

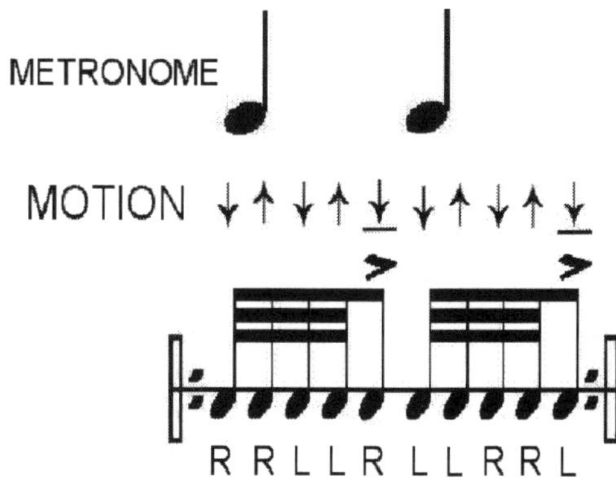

#4 The 7 Stroke Roll

This is a non-alternating roll. Meaning you start with your R.H. and on the repeat you'll start with the RH. After you master the RH lead switch to the LH.

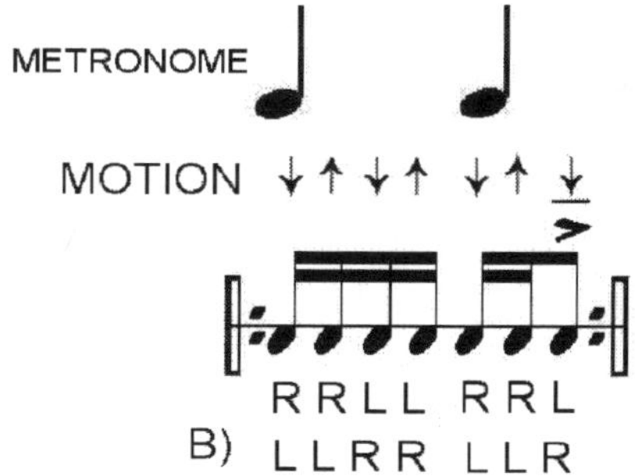

#5 The 9 Stroke Roll

This roll is in ¾ and it's alternating.

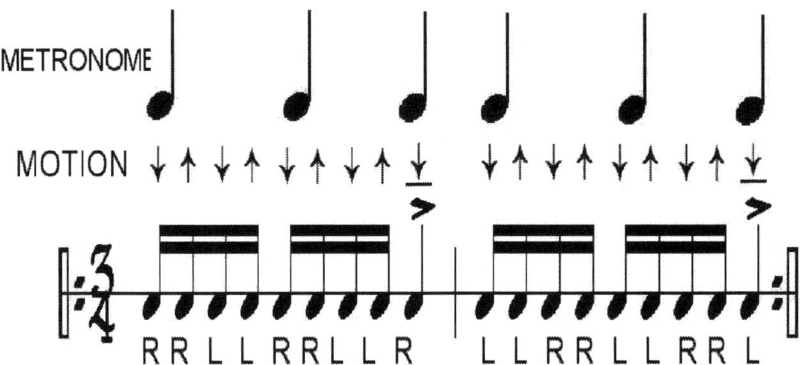

#6 The 10 Stroke Roll

Another ¾ non-alternating roll.

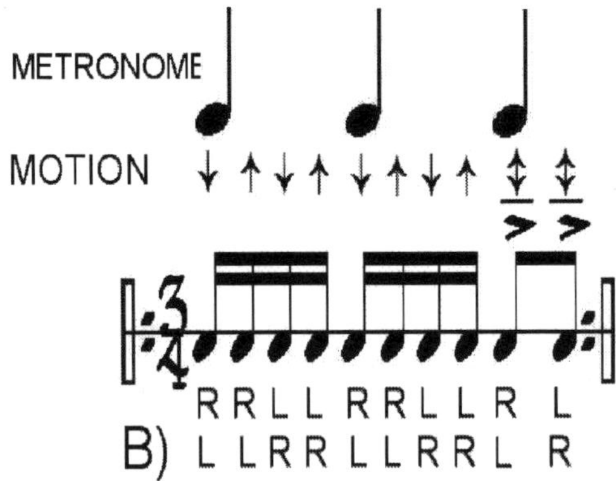

#7 The 11 Stroke Roll

The last ¾ non alternating roll

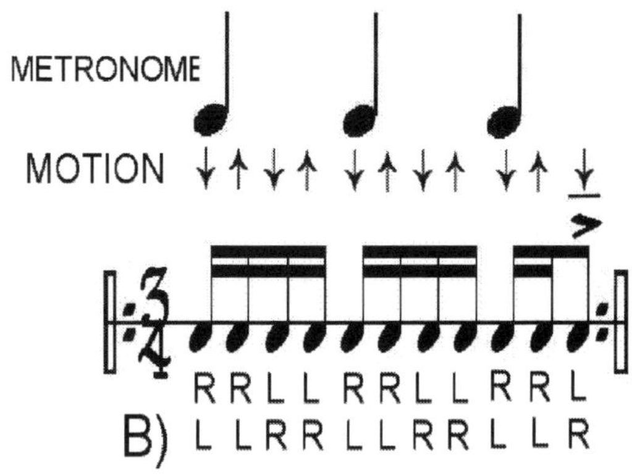

#8 The 13 Stroke Roll

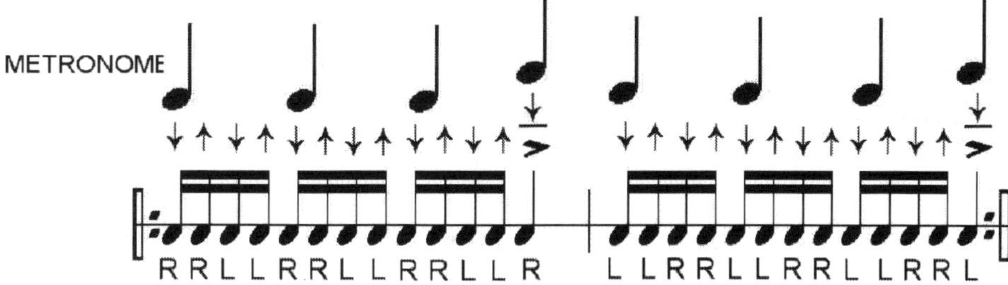

#9 The 15 Stroke Roll

The last of the roll rudiments. Remember you can buzz all these rolls by simply
squeezing the fulcrum to create a multiple bounce instead of an DOWN/UP.

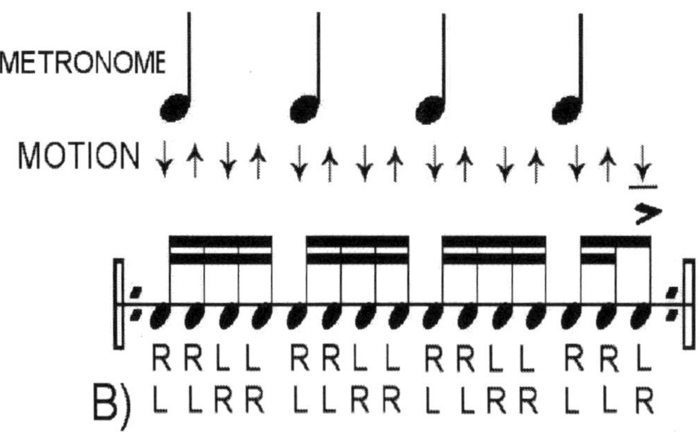

RRLL RRLL RRLL RRL
B) LLRR LLRR LLRR LLR

#10 The Paradiddle

Another commonly known rudiment it has the best of both worlds. Start with a DOWN stroke ACCENT in the R.H., then an UP stroke in the L.H. and finally 2 bounces with the R.H. Then reverse the sequence.

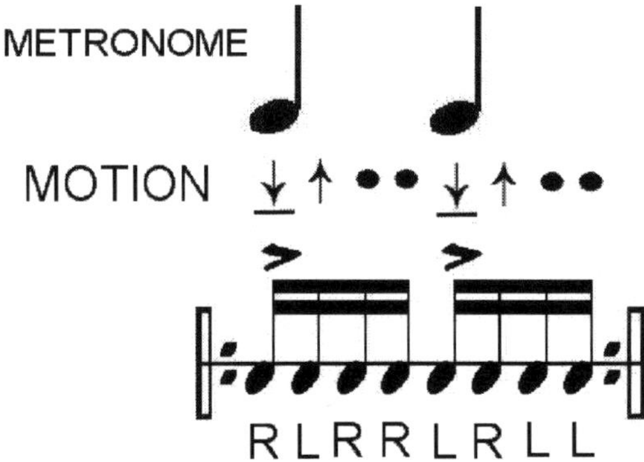

RLRRLRLL

#11 The Double Paradiddle

Same as the latter just add 2 single strokes this time you use the FULL accented stroke to start.

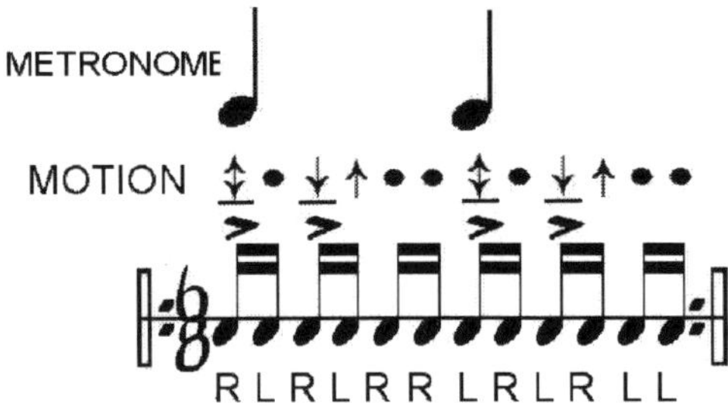

RLRLRR LRLR LL

#12 The Triple Paradiddle

Again adding 2 more FULL accented single strokes.

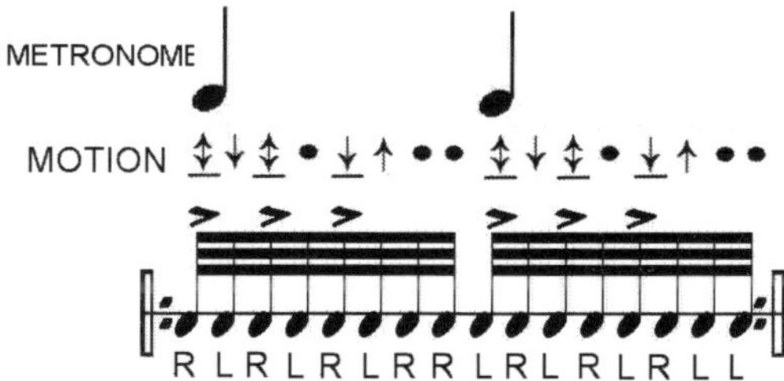

#13 The Flam

The non alternating Flam is played with 2 DOWN strokes one staggered before the other then 2 UP strokes. If you think about it it's a Double Stroke Roll but the 2 notes are played together at different heights.

Non- Alternating

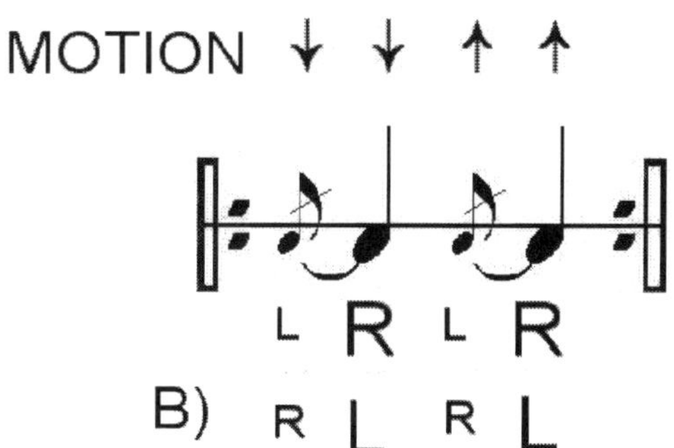

Alternating

Start with an UP stroke and a DOWN stroke staggered. When you pick up speed it feels exactly like a Double Stroke Roll that flams.

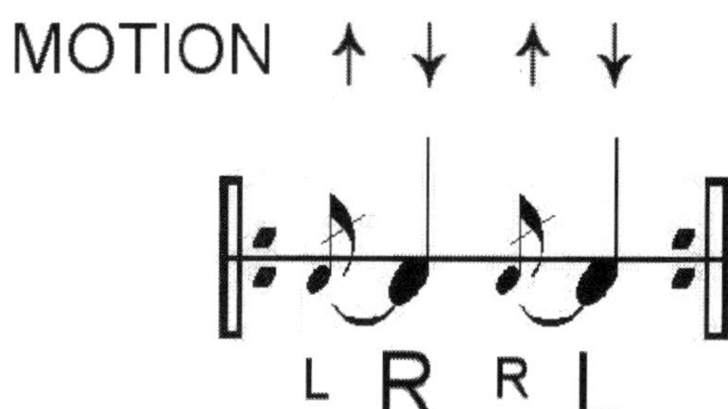

#14 The Flam Tap

The Alternating version is a 3 Stroke Roll staggered into itself.

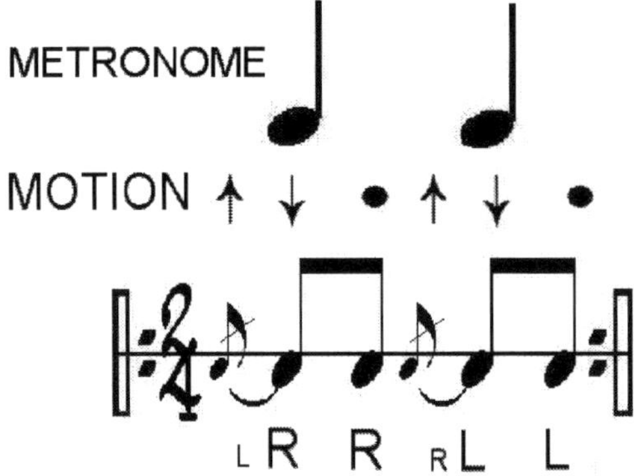

Non-Alternating

This has two DOWN/UP motions going on at the same time. The Flam grace note is played half time of the main notes.

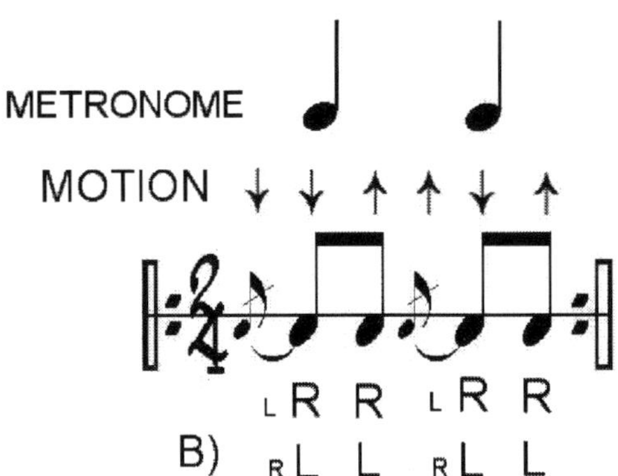

#15 The Flam Accent

An alternating Triplet rhythm with a Flam in the beginning...... sounds like a great night out.

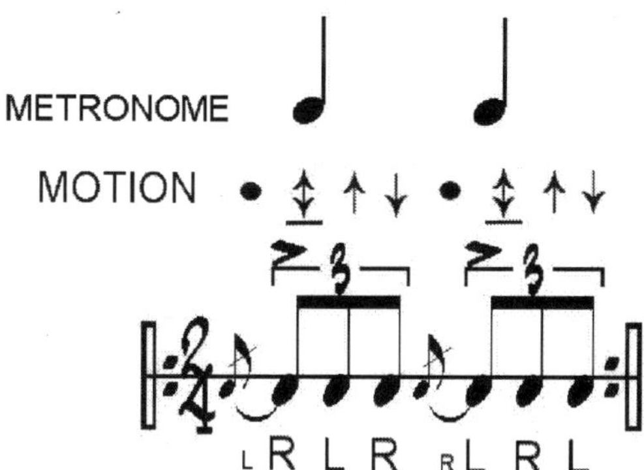

#16 The Flam Paradiddle

The Flam Paradiddle, as you've learned before requires a 4 stroke roll in the middle of the phrase. Study it well.

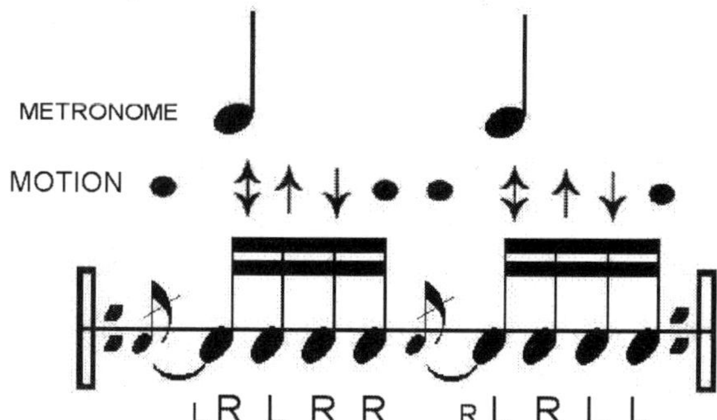

#17 The Flamacue

The names they come up with. The Flam starts with a grace note UP stroke and a main note BOUNCE.

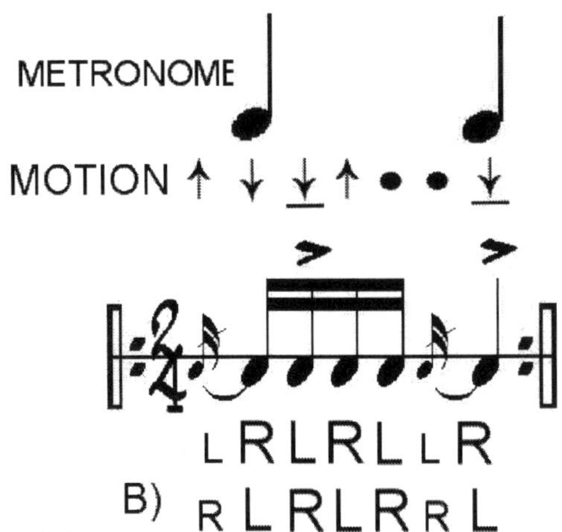

#18 The Ruff

The Ruff is like a Flam but you double the grace note. The grace note has no musical value it's played a hair before the main note. The non-alternating version has a DOWN/UP motion playing half time from each other.

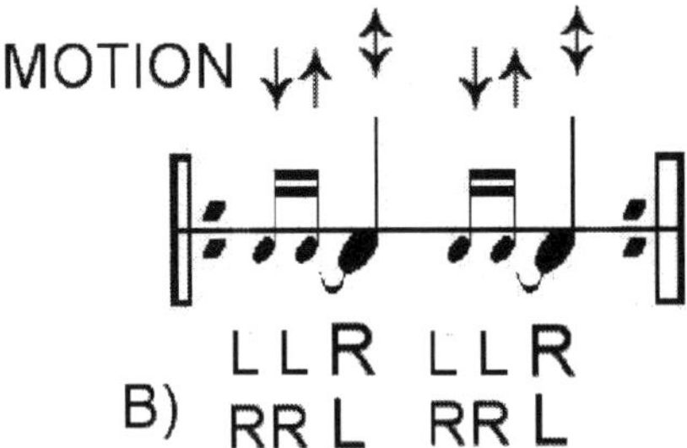

Alternating
Same motion as the Alt Flam but add 1 note to the grace.

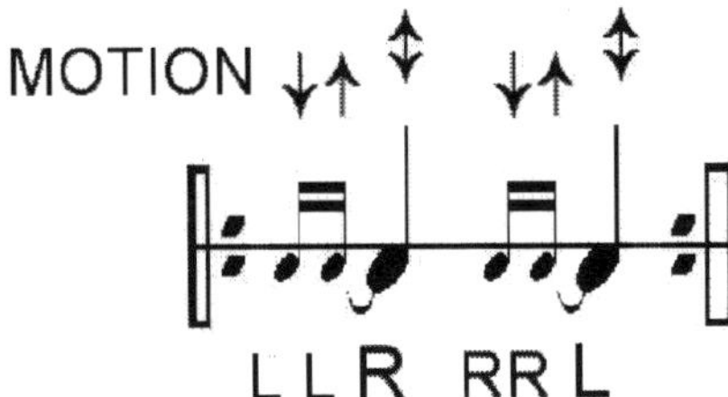

#19 The Drag

I can hear the jokes now. It's a Double Stroke Roll with ruffs thrown in to make it...... A Drag!

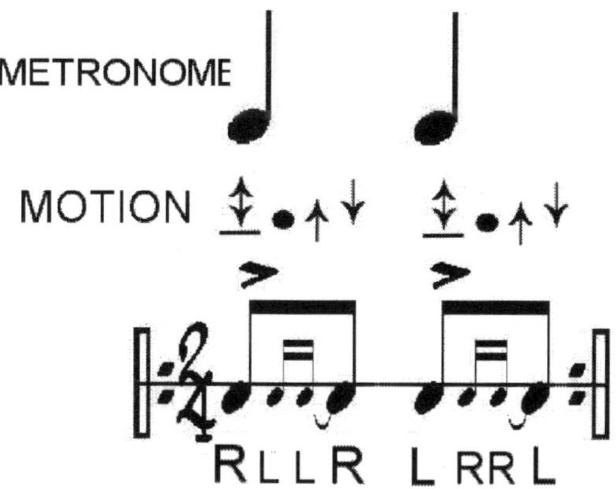

#20 The Double Drag

This is in ¾ and you double the Ruff.

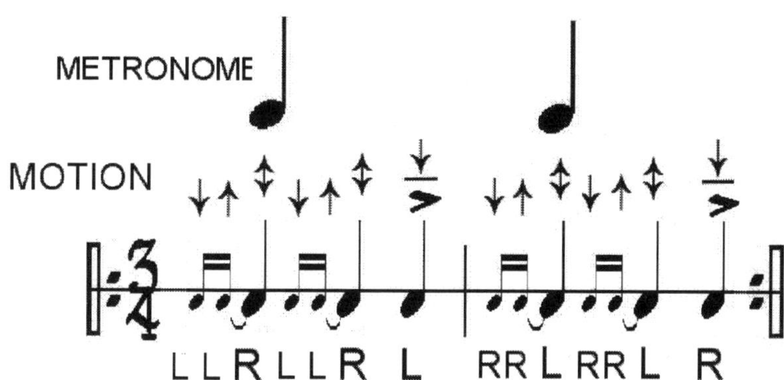

#21 The Drag Paradiddle

I know you're thinking"enough with the Paradiddle already!" But I did warn you it's a cornerstone of the rudiments. In 3, a 1... a 2... and a...

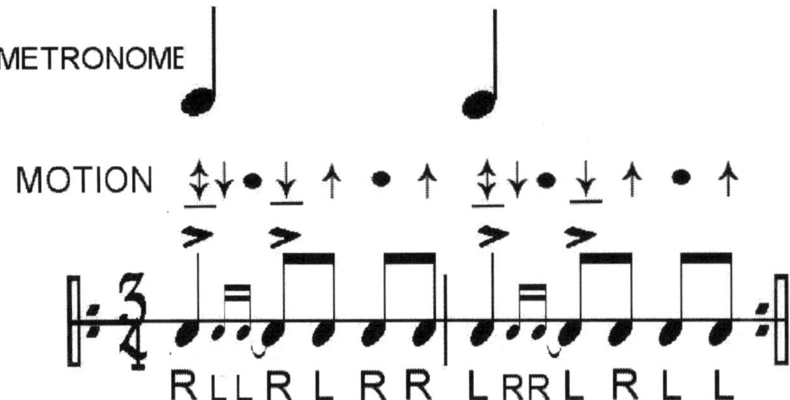

#22 The Double Drag Paradiddle

Yep I said it....

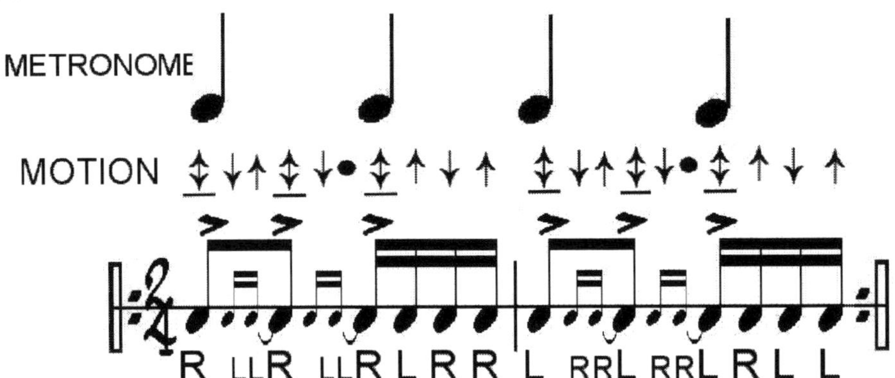

#23 The Ratamacue

This rudiment sounds like it's said. Start with a ruff then a Triplet and an accent.

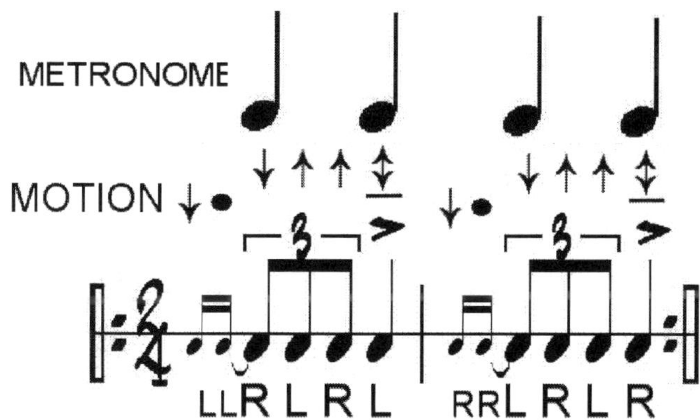

#24 The Double Ratamacue

Same as the latter just add another Ruff at the start.

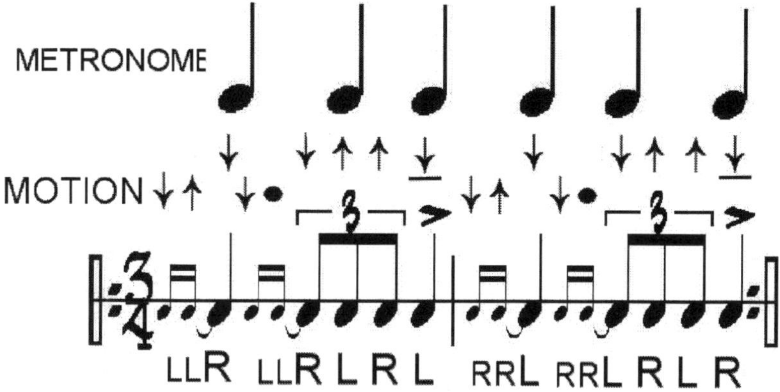

#25 Lesson 25

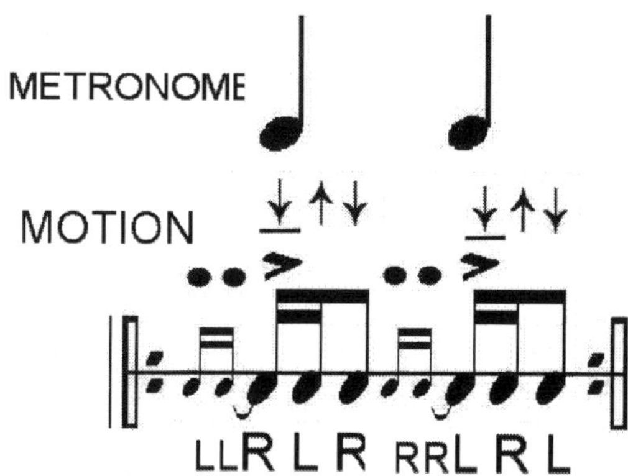

#26 The Triple Ratamacue

Just like the Triple Lindy seen on Coney Island Pier so long ago.... Three ruffs, a Triplet and an accented note finish it up.

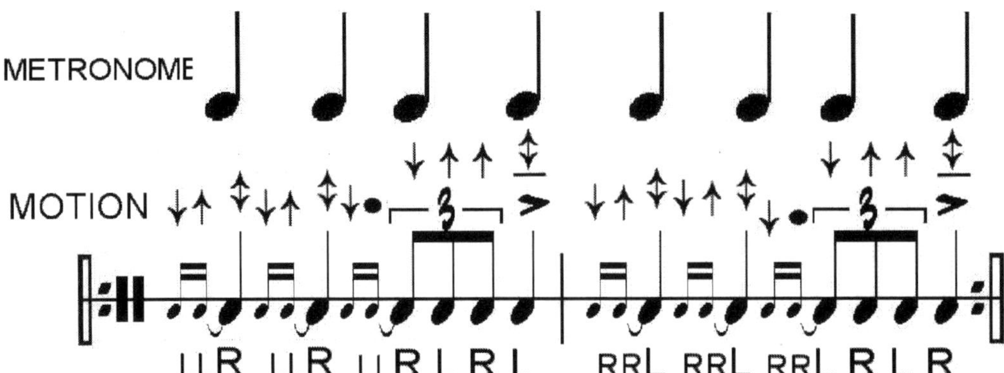

Using the rudiments, along with the motion and conceptual ideas presented in this book shall give you a very good foundation to build on. Remember to constantly challenge yourself with ideas and rhythmical phrases.

UNIQUELY INTERESTING MUSIC

Made in the USA
Charleston, SC
28 October 2010